General and Complete Disarmament
Comprehensive Study on Nuclear Weapons
Report of the Secretary-General

By resolution 33/91 D of 16 December 1978, the General Assembly requested the Secretary-General, with the assistance of qualified experts, to carry out a comprehensive study on nuclear weapons.

Pursuant to that resolution, the Secretary-General appointed a Group of Experts on a Comprehensive Study on Nuclear Weapons, which met from 9 to 13 July and 15 to 19 October 1979 and from 23 January to 1 February, 21 to 25 April and 7 to 12 July 1980.

By a letter dated 12 July 1980, the Chairman of the Group of Experts transmitted to the Secretary-General the report which was thereby submitted to the General Assembly.

Nuclear Weapons

*Report of the Secretary-General
of the United Nations*

Autumn  Press

NUCLEAR WEAPONS is the complete Report of the Secretary-General of the United Nations entitled *General and Complete Disarmament: Comprehensive Study on Nuclear Weapons: Report of the Secretary-General*, which was presented to the General Assembly in the Fall of 1980. All rights reserved.

Published with the authorization and cooperation of the United Nations

Published by Autumn Press, Inc.
with editorial offices at
1318 Beacon Street
Brookline, Massachusetts 02146

ISBN 0-914398-45-8, cloth
ISBN 0-914398-33-4, paper
Library of Congress Catalog Number: 81-66775

Printed in the United States of America
Typeset at dnh, Cambridge, Massachusetts

Book design & typography by Michael Fender
Art consultant: Michael Prendergast

Contents

Foreword

By its resolution 33/91 D of 16 December 1978, the General Assembly requested the Secretary-General, with the assistance of qualified experts, to carry out a comprehensive study providing factual information on present nuclear arsenals, trends in the technological development of nuclear-weapon systems, the effects of their use and the implications for international security as well as for negotiations on disarmament of: (a) the doctrines of deterrence and other theories concerning nuclear weapons; and (b) the continued quantitative increase and qualitative improvement and development of nuclear-weapon systems.

In pursuance of the resolution, a group of qualified experts was appointed after consultations with Member States. The Group held five sessions between July 1979 and July 1980.

The experts, in their personal capacities, have submitted to the Secretary-General a unanimous report containing their considered views on a subject-matter whose great importance is only matched by the intricate and complex nature of the various aspects involved. The report constitutes, in effect, the first United Nations study to be undertaken on the subject of nuclear weapons in over 10 years, since the publications of the previous United Nations study entitled *Effects of the Possible Use of Nuclear Weapons and the Security and Economic Implications for States of the Acquisition and Further Development of These Weapons.*[1] In its resolution 33/91 D, which contained the mandate for the present study, the General Assembly noted that many important developments have taken place in the nuclear arms sector since the earlier study and

that the new study would make a valuable contribution to the dissemination of factual information and to international understanding of the
issues involved. In this context, it needs once again to be emphasized
that nuclear disarmament continues to be the overriding priority in the
effort to restrain the armaments race. The tenth special session of the
General Assembly, devoted to disarmament, which was held in 1978,
gave tangible recognition to this reality when in paragraph 47 of its Final
Document (resolution S-10/2) it noted that nuclear weapons pose the
greatest danger to mankind and to the survival of civilization and under-
scored the need to halt and reverse the nuclear arms race in all its aspects
in order to avert the danger of war involving nuclear weapons. Since the
ultimate goal in this context is the complete elimination of nuclear
weapons, careful study and continuous assessment of nuclear-weapon
problems are clearly required to assist the international community in
achieving progress in this field. In this light, also, the new study
assumes a rightful place as a vehicle for disseminating further information on a topic of such vital importance to all.

The Secretary-General wishes to thank the experts for their unanimous report which, in pursuance of paragraph 4 of resolution 33/91 D,
he hereby submits to the General Assembly for its consideration. It
should be noted that the observations and recommendations contained
in the report are those of the experts. In this connexion, the Secretary-
General would like to point out that in the complex field of disarmament matters, in many instances he is not in a position to pass judgement on all aspects of the work accomplished by experts.

THE SECRETARY-GENERAL
of the UNITED NATIONS

UNITED NATIONS NATIONS UNIES

LETTER OF TRANSMITTAL

12 July 1980

His Excellency
Mr. Kurt Waldheim
Secretary-General of the United Nations

Sir,

I have the honour to submit herewith the report of the Group of Experts on a Comprehensive Study on Nuclear Weapons which was appointed by you in pursuance of paragraph 1 of General Assembly resolution 33/91 D of 16 December 1978.

The Experts appointed by you were the following:

Mr. F. K. A. Allotey
PRO-VICE-CHANCELLOR
Dean of Faculty of Science
University of Science and
   Technology
Kumasi, Ghana

Mr. Fathih K. Bouayad-Agha
MINISTER PLENIPOTENTIARY
Secretariat General
Ministry of Foreign Affairs
Algeria

Colonel Milutin Civić
SPECIAL ADVISER ON
   DISARMAMENT
Ministry of Foreign Affairs
Belgrade, Yugoslavia

Mr. Francisco Correa-Villalobos
COUNSELLOR
*Permanent Mission of Mexico to
   the United Nations*
New York

x

Mr. Ryukichi Imai
General Manager, Engineering Dept.
The Japan Atomic Power Co.
Tokyo, Japan
AMBASSADOR EXTRAORDINARY
AND PLENIPOTENTIARY
Ambassador of Japan in Kuwait

Mr. Albert Legault
DIRECTOR GENERAL OF THE
QUEBEC CENTER FOR
INTERNATIONAL RELATIONS
University of Laval
Faculty of Social Sciences
Quebec, Canada

Mr. Jamsheed K. A. Marker
AMBASSADOR EXTRAORDINARY
AND PLENIPOTENTIARY
*Permanent Representative of
Pakistan to the United Nations
Office at Geneva*

Mr. Jose Maria Otegui
FIRST SECRETARY OF EMBASSY
Ministry of Foreign Affairs
Buenos Aires, Argentina

Mr. Alan Oxley
NUCLEAR AND DEFENCE DIVISION
Department of Foreign Affairs
Canberra A. C. T., Australia

Mr. Anders I. Thunborg
AMBASSADOR EXTRAORDINARY
AND PLENIPOTENTIARY
*Permanent Representative of
Sweden to the United
Nations*

Mr. Gheorghe Tinca
FIRST SECRETARY
Ministry of Foreign Affairs
Bucharest, Romania

Mr. M. A. Vellodi
ADVISER
Department of Atomic Energy
Bombay, India

The report was prepared between July 1979 and July 1980, during which period the Group held five sessions, from 9 to 13 July 1979 in New York, 15 to 19 October 1979 in Geneva, and 23 January to 1 February 1980, 21 to 25 April 1980, and 7 to 12 July 1980 in New York.

At the first two sessions of the Group, Mr. Nacereddine Haffad participated as an expert from Algeria and Professor Owen Harries participated as an expert from Australia.

The members of the Group of Experts wish to express their appreciation for the valuable assistance which they received from members of the Secretariat of the United Nations. They wish, in particular, to convey their thanks to Mr. Allessandro Corradini, Centre for Disarmament, who served as Secretary of the Group during the first two sessions; to Mr. Sohrab Kheradi, also from the Centre, who served as Secretary during the three subsequent sessions; and to Professor Richard L. Garwin, who served in his private capacity as consultant to the Secretariat on chapters 2 and 3 of the report.

I have been requested by the Group of Experts, as its Chairman, to submit to you on its behalf its report, which was unanimously approved.

Accept, Sir, the assurance of my highest consideration.

Anders I. Thunborg
Chairman of the Group of Experts on a Comprehensive Study on Nuclear Weapons

Nuclear Weapons

I

Introduction

THE FINAL DOCUMENT of the Tenth Special Session of the General Assembly was adopted by consensus on 30 June 1978 (resolution). That document set out, for the first time in the history of the United Nations, an agreed Programme of Action on disarmament containing priorities and measures that States should undertake as a matter of urgency. First among the priorities and most urgent among the measures advocated stands nuclear disarmament. The reasons given in paragraph 47 of the Final Document are that:

> "Nuclear weapons pose the greatest danger to mankind and to the survival of civilization. It is essential to halt and reverse the nuclear arms race in all its aspects in order to avert the danger of war involving nuclear weapons. The ultimate goal in this context is the complete elimination of nuclear weapons."

At the tenth special session the General Assembly also pointed to the important need for the United Nations to increase the dissemination of information about the armaments race and all matters related to disarmament with the full co-operation of its Member States. The question of nuclear disarmament is foremost in this respect and the present report can therefore be seen as a concrete effort to fulfil an important provision of the Final Document.

Subsequently, the General Assembly adopted resolution 33/91 D, the operative paragraphs of which read as follows:

"1. *Requests* the Secretary-General, with the assistance of qualified experts,[1] to carry out a comprehensive study providing factual information on present nuclear arsenals, trends in the technological development of nuclear-weapon systems, the effects of their use and the implications for international security as well as for negotiations on disarmament of:

   (a) The doctrines of deterrence and other theories concerning nuclear weapons;

   (b) The continued quantitative increase and qualitative improvement and development of nuclear-weapon systems;

"2. *Recommends* that the study, while aiming at being as comprehensive as possible, should be based on open material and such further information that Member States may wish to make available for the purpose of the study;

"3. *Invites* all Governments to co-operate with the Secretary-General so that the objectives of the study may be achieved;

"4. *Requests* the Secretary-General to submit the final report to the General Assembly at its thirty-fifth session."

The present study is the result of action taken as a consequence of the adoption of resolution 33/91 D. It follows up the previous United Nations study on nuclear weapons, carried out more than 12 years ago: *Effects of the Possible Use of Nuclear Weapons and the Security and Economic Implications for States of the Acquisition and Further Development of These Weapons.*[2] It is of interest to recall here the conclusion of that report, which stated:

1968

"Since the sense of insecurity on the part of nations is the cause of the arms race, which in turn enhances that very insecurity, and in so far as nuclear armaments are the end of a spectrum which begins with conventional weapons, the problem of reversing the trend of a rapidly worsening world situation calls for a basic reappraisal of all interrelated factors. The solution of the problem of ensuring security cannot be found in an increase in the number of States possessing nuclear weapons or, indeed, in the retention of nuclear weapons by the Powers currently possessing them. An Agreement to prevent the spread of nuclear weapons as recommended by the United Nations, freely negotiated and genuinely observed, would therefore be a powerful step in the right direction, as would also an agreement on the reduction of existing nuclear arsenals. Security for all countries of the world must be sought through the elimination of all stockpiles of nuclear weapons and the banning of their use, by way of general and complete disarmament.

"A comprehensive test ban treaty, prohibiting the underground testing of nuclear devices, would also contribute to the objectives of non-proliferation and would clearly help to slow down the nuclear arms race. So would effective measures safeguarding the security of non-nuclear countries. Nuclear-weapon-free zones additional to those of Antarctica and Latin America, covering the maximum geo-graphical extent possible and taking into account other measures of arms control and disarmament, would equally be of major assistance.

"These measures are mentioned neither to argue the case for them nor to set them in any order of priority. What the analysis of the whole problem shows is that any one of them, or any combination of them, could help inhibit the further multiplication of nuclear weapons Powers or the further elaboration of existing nuclear arsenals and so help to ensure national and world security. But it must be realized that these measures of arms limitation, however desirable, cannot of themselves eliminate the threat of nuclear conflict. They should be regarded not as ends sufficient in themselves but only as measures which could lead to the reduction of the level of nuclear armaments and the lessening of tension in the world and the eventual elimina-tion of nuclear armaments. All countries have a clear interest in the evolution of a world which allows of peaceful and stable coexistence. Non-nuclear weapon countries, as well as those which possess nuclear weapons, need to work in concert, creating conditions in which there should be free access to materials, equipment and infor-mation for achieving all the peaceful benefits of atomic energy, and for promoting international security.

"This report gives the bare outline of the disasters which could be associated with the use of nuclear weapons. It discusses the nature and variety of the economic burden they impose. And it unhesitat-ingly concludes from the considerations that have been set out that whatever the path to national and international security in the future, it is certainly not to be found in the further spread and elaboration of nuclear weapons. The threat of the immeasurable disaster which could befall mankind were nuclear war ever to erupt, whether by miscalculation or by mad intent, is so real that informed people the world over understandably become impatient for measures of disarmament additional to the few measures of arms limitation that have already been agreed to—the limited ban on testing, the prohibition of nuclear weapons in outer space, and the nuclear-free zone of Latin America. International agreement against the further proliferation of nuclear weapons and agreements on measures of arms control and disarmament will promote the security of all countries. The United Nations has the overriding responsibility in this field. The more effective it becomes in action, the more powerful its authority, the greater becomes the assurance for man's future. And the longer the world waits, the more nuclear arsenals grow, the greater and more difficult becomes the eventual task."

In the 12 years that have elapsed since the submission of the previous report, the nuclear arms race has continued unabated. Notwithstanding the fact that some measures of arms control have been adopted, no measures of nuclear disarmament have been agreed. Furthermore, numerous important technological and other developments have occurred which motivate not only an updating but a new and comprehensive review of the entire problem. Among such developments may be mentioned the anti-ballistic missiles (ABM), multiple independently targetable re-entry vehicles (MIRV), cruise missiles, mobile land-based missiles, the "neutron bomb", the growing nuclear power industry, the miniaturization of nuclear weapons and the simpler methods of production developed, the increased risk of dissemination of these weapons to various nations and subnational groups, etc. The list could be made longer. In these same years, the total number of strategic nuclear warheads has increased from 4,500 to at least 9,200 for the United States and from 1,000 to at least 6,000 for the USSR. There would thus seem to exist a very strong case for a new report on all aspects of nuclear weapons in order to provide accurate and authoritative information to as wide a public as possible.

Against this background it must be noted, with regret and concern, that the nuclear-weapon States, and in particular the two
super-Powers, have withheld their participation in the work of
the Group of Experts. The Chairman of the Group has nevertheless kept the super-Powers informed of the preparation of this
report.

One basic difficulty in the work on this report has been the
absence, in many cases, of officially available data on nuclear
weapons and related questions. In consequence the Group has in
several instances relied on other available data, in each instance
providing the relevant reference in order to facilitate for the
reader an understanding of the factual basis of the report.

The present report is organized in eight chapters. Chapters II to
IV are of a technical nature and refer to existing and future
nuclear-weapon capabilities as well as the effects of nuclear weapons. Chapters V to VII contain a description and analyses of the
implications for security and disarmament of the development of
nuclear weapons as well as the doctrines for their use. A concluding summary appears in chapter VIII. Appendix I contains a technical description of nuclear-weapon effects. Appendix II sets
forth "Security assurances" by the nuclear-weapon States as presented to the Committee on Disarmament in 1980. Appendix III
outlines the characteristics of some important nuclear-weapon
systems.

II

Factual Information on Present Nuclear Arsenals

THE EXACT NUMBER of nuclear warheads in the world today is probably not known by any single person or institution, and estimates cannot be verified officially. Published figures indicate, however, that the total may be in excess of 40,000. In explosive power these warheads are reported to range from about 100 tons up to more than 20 million tons equivalent of chemical high explosive. The largest weapon ever tested released an energy approximately 4,000 times that of the atomic bomb that levelled Hiroshima, and there is in principle no upper limit to the explosive yield that may be attained. The total strength of present nuclear arsenals may be equivalent to about 1 million Hiroshima bombs, i.e., some 13,000 million tons of TNT. It is often pointed out that this is equivalent to more than 3 tons for every man, woman and child on the earth. The arsenals of the United States and the Soviet Union contain most of these weapons, with the known remainder belonging to China, France and the United Kingdom.

A measure of the resources claimed by nuclear-weapon programmes is the amount of natural uranium they consume. It is estimated that 4 to 5 per cent of the uranium believed to be available in the ground in the United States and Canada (between 2 and 3 million metric tons) has already been processed for the extraction of enriched uranium-235 for military purposes. Additional uranium has been converted to plutonium, of which the bulk so far has been used to fabricate nuclear weapons.

In terms of defence expenditure, the budgetary demands for equipment and labour to make these vast numbers of nuclear warheads are now stated to be in the range of $2,000 to $2,500 million annually for the United States and believed to be about the same for the Soviet Union. This may be less than 1 per cent of the total defence budgets of the two super-Powers, but the delivery systems claim 10 times as much and when research and development costs are included, the amount for nuclear forces comes to about 20 per cent of the entire defence budget, according to United States estimates.

The nuclear weapon

The energy released by a nuclear weapon originates in the nucleus of the atom. In the fission bomb, the process involved is the splitting of uranium or plutonium nuclei into lighter fragments, fission products. In a thermonuclear or hydrogen bomb, nuclei of heavy hydrogen isotopes—deuterium and tritium—are fused together at the very high temperatures triggered through the fission process.

The speed of the nuclear reactions is enormous. Both in a fission and a fusion explosive, the entire nuclear energy is released in about one millionth of a second. With today's technique, it is thus possible to release by one weapon more energy in one microsecond than that from all conventional weapons in all wars of history.

In order to sustain the chain reaction in a fission explosion, it is necessary to have more than a certain minimum amount of fissile material, the critical mass. This mass depends upon the purity and density of the material, its geometrical shape, the possible presence of neutron reflecting materials and other factors. The fissile material has to be brought together very quickly if the weapon is to explode with great force. Conventional explosives are used for this purpose and the fissile material put together, with or without compression, to a size which, for a plutonium bomb, needs to

be no larger in volume than a man's fist. At this time the chain
reaction is initiated. The 1968 United Nations study on nuclear
weapons set 8 kg. of plutonium containing 90 to 95 per cent of
plutonium-239 and 25 kg. of highly enriched uranium-235 as the
amounts necessary to achieve an explosion with a yield corresponding to 20 kt. of high explosive. Depending on the design
sophistication and with high quality material, this mass can range
from 15 to 25 kg. for uranium-235 and from 4 to 8 kg. for plu-
tonium-239.[3]

If a fission device is accompanied by the heavy isotopes of
hydrogen, the high temperature and pressure triggered by the
explosion can cause the fusion of these isotopes into heavier ones,
thereby releasing vast amounts of energy. Even though one
fusion reaction releases less energy than one fission reaction, the
amount of energy released per kilogram of nuclear explosive
material can be more than four times as large in a fusion device as
in a fission device.

The energy is usually expressed in units of kiloton (kt.) or
megaton (Mt.) corresponding to the energy release in a thousand
or a million metric tons of TNT (trinitrotoluene). The atomic
bomb dropped on Hiroshima on 6 August 1945 derived its energy
from a chain reaction fissioning the nuclei of uranium-235 atoms
and had a yield of 13 kt. The critical size was achieved using a
"gun" to shoot one piece of uranium into another. In contrast, the
Nagasaki bomb of 9 August 1945 utilized plutonium-239 and had
a yield of 22 kt. The plutonium was arranged as a spherical shell
which was crushed together by a surrounding shell of chemical
explosive. This is referred to as a "nuclear implosion weapon".

The design of a thermonuclear weapon is publicly less well
known in all its details. The energy released comes both from the
fission "trigger" and the fusion materials. There may also be
added a considerable amount of fission energy by surrounding
the fusion weapon with a shell of uranium-238. The fission reactions give rise to much larger amounts of radioactivity than the
fusion reactions. For this reason, thermonuclear weapons are
sometimes spoken of as "clean" or "dirty", depending on what

fraction of their total energy release derives from fission. Even a "clean" weapon generates some radioactivity, however, both as debris from the fission trigger and tritium and as "induced activity" caused by the massive outflux of neutrons from the explosion.

Long-range delivery systems

The nuclear explosive can be carried to the intended target by various delivery vehicles. Among them, the land-based intercontinental ballistic missile (ICBM) is considered highly reliable and accurate, i.e., a large fraction is ready to be launched at any time and would be able to reach and destroy their targets. The carriers are multistage rockets with an intercontinental range of up to 13,000 km. or 7,000 nautical miles (one nmi is 1.852 km.), based in "hardened" silos and linked up to an elaborate system of command and control. The term "ballistic" derives from the motion of the re-entry vehicle (RV) which is governed by inertia and gravity after separation from the rocket. The shape of the RV is chosen to minimize drag upon re-entry into the atmosphere, so as to maintain accuracy under variable winds and to render the high-speed RV difficult to defend against. The transit time of the ICBM over its intercontinental range is about 30 minutes. Figure I indicates the size of the areas covered by such long-range missiles.

The rocket may carry one or several warheads, which may be independently targeted. The multiple independently targetable re-entry vehicle (MIRV) system was developed by the United States in the late 1960s and is deployed also by the Soviet Union. In a MIRVed system, the separate re-entry vehicles are usually carried on a "bus" which releases the RVs one by one after making preselected changes in speed and orientation so as to direct the RVs to their separate targets. These RVs can reportedly land inside an area of perhaps 150 km. by 500 km. Thus, they are not as completely independent in arrival time or location as they would be were they on different ICBMs, and they provide less targeting flexibility.

Figure I. Examples of ICBM Ranges

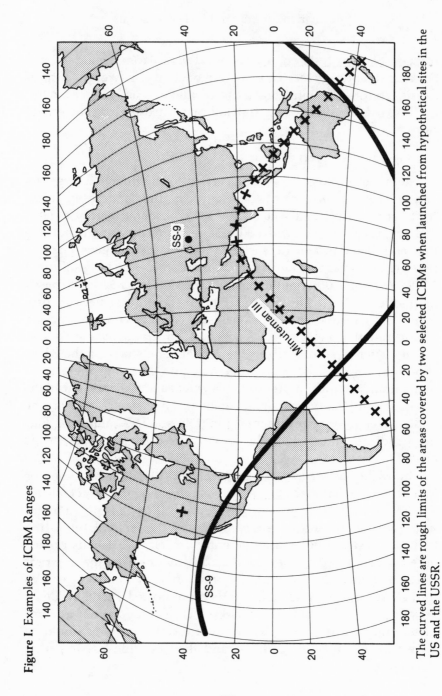

The curved lines are rough limits of the areas covered by two selected ICBMs when launched from hypothetical sites in the US and the USSR.

12

With increasing missile accuracy and many RVs per missile, MIRV has raised the spectre that a fraction of one side's ICBM forces may in a "first strike" destroy the opponent's ICBMs still housed in their hardened silos. This would be possible with sufficient accuracy and reliability of the attacking RVs, and if the ICBMs to be attacked were not launched before they were destroyed. This situation is therefore considered to be potentially unstable, since in time of crisis each side may consider launching its missiles rather than risk their destruction.

If a target is vulnerable to a particular pressure level of the air blast, its destruction may be achieved within a certain maximum area around the point of detonation. The size of this area increases with the weapon yield (e.g., by a factor 4 for an 8-fold increase in yield or a factor 100 for a 1,000-fold increase in yield). By contrast, the area of destruction due to blast increases in proportion to the number of weapons. This means in practice that the destruction is increased by increasing the number of warheads and lowering their individual RV yield; i.e., one large warhead is not so effective as several smaller ones of the same total yield spread out over the target area. This is also illustrated by Fig. II.

In order to destroy a "hard" target an attacker will use a powerful warhead, unless he has a missile of high accuracy. Missile accuracy is usually given in terms of the circular error probable (CEP), defined as the distance from the target within which, on the average, half the re-entry vehicles will land if aimed directly at the target. For example, a 1 Mt. nuclear warhead may be needed on a missile with a CEP of 1 km. in order to destroy a particular hardened structure. The same effect could result from a 125 kt. warhead with a 0.5 km. CEP missile accuracy, or a 40 kt. warhead with 0.33 km. CEP. Megatonnage alone is thus a very misleading measure of one side's capability. Of equal or more importance is missile accuracy.

Definite CEP values for different existing missile systems are not available, for reasons both of secrecy and, presumably, insufficient basic knowledge. However, several open sources give estimates for many of these systems. The indications are that both

Figure II. Relationship Between Weapon Yield and Area Destroyed by Blast

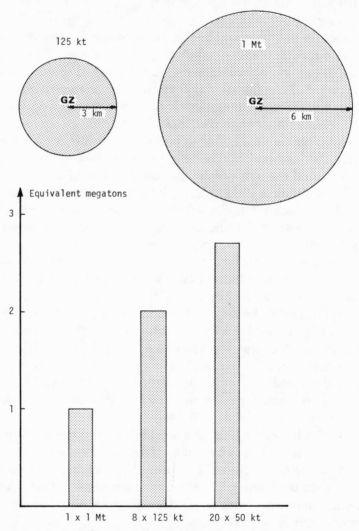

The circles illustrate how the size of the area destroyed by blast increases with weapon yield. This is accounted for by the introduction of "equivalent mega-tonnage" (see also note 22). In the lower part of the figure are three examples of the equivalent megatonnage when the nominal yield 1 Mt is delivered in three different ways.

United States and Soviet ICBMs are approaching a CEP of about 200 m.

Another delivery vehicle for nuclear weapons is the submarine-launched ballistic missile (SLBM). Even though an individual submarine may be vulnerable to attack, this system as a whole has the powerful advantage of virtual invulnerability as long as the submarines are travelling undetected under the ocean surface. At present, no nation is known to have an anti-submarine capability that threatens this invulnerability. In comparison with the ICBM, however, the SLBMs are considered to have a more tenuous communication link with the national command authority, particularly under wartime conditions. Also, they are for the time being less accurate than their land-based counterpart, partly because of the uncertainty of the submarine's determination of its location, orientation and velocity. Thus the SLBM is not at present suited to attack small "hard" targets (e.g., missile silos), but could be utilized against larger and "softer" targets, such as military bases, air fields and population centres. They are thus not considered destabilizing in the sense that the accurate MIRVed ICBMs may be. However, because of the possibility that the attacking submarine may come quite close to some targets, warning of an attack could be considerably less than for ICBM missiles. The SLBMs are therefore considered to be a serious threat to bombers which might have time to fly out from under an ICBM attack.

A third method of nuclear-weapon delivery, emphasized more by the United States than the USSR, is by long-range bomber. With sufficient warning, the United States bomber force would carry between one fourth and one third of all deliverable United States strategic nuclear weapons, adding up to perhaps half the total megatonnage, while the Soviet strategic nuclear payload is concentrated in its ICBMs. The bombers could carry either gravity bombs or various aerodynamic or "cruise" missiles. The latter can be fired from a "stand-off" position, i.e., without the bomber penetrating the enemy's air defences, which enhances the operational survivability of the system. The manned bomber force may be recalled after dispatch, or retargeted en route. This flexibility in addition to the large payload possible is considered the main advantage of the strategic bomber force, while the disadvantages are its vulnerability and low speed, as compared with ICBMs.

Cruise missiles, as defined by the SALT II treaty, are "unmanned, self-propelled guided weapon delivery vehicles which sustain flight through the use of aerodynamic lift over most of their flight path". With an advanced navigation and guidance system, such as those described in chapter III, the cruise missile may have a CEP of less than 100 m. With a nuclear warhead of moderate yield, it would be capable of destroying the hardest targets. The speed is subsonic and the flight time may be many hours. Because of this, it has been maintained that the cruise missile should not be considered as a first strike weapon.

Technological development has increased the effectiveness of nuclear weapons in the 12 years since the earlier United Nations report, to some extent by the continued evolution of the nuclear explosive but mainly by improvements in the accuracy and flexibility of delivery. To retain in 1980 the same destructive capability, particularly against hard targets, as in 1968, fewer weapons would thus be needed. As has already been pointed out, however, nuclear weapons have greatly increased in numbers since 1968.

Intelligence, command, control and communications

The nuclear-weapon States have instituted systems—reportedly of a very elaborate nature—to maintain control over their large nuclear forces. These systems would have a dual purpose: to prevent unintentional or unauthorized release of weapons and to ensure that decisions to use nuclear weapons are not based on false information, but also to ensure that such a decision, when made, is carried out rapidly and reliably.

Neither the basic structure nor the technical details of such intelligence, command, control and communications systems are publicly known. It is obvious, however, that they could be designed to serve either a centralized or a decentralized command authority. It is also obvious—from several press reports of false alarms over the years—that the systems are not infallible. For this reason there is a growing concern that control may some day fail, under the influence of, for example, a false message or a misunderstood command, and that nuclear war is thus triggered inadvertently.

The main strategic arsenals of the super-Powers[4]

In the proposed SALT II treaty[5] between the United States and the Soviet Union, there is an exchange of data on the strategic nuclear forces of both sides. The forces in question are those with capability to threaten the super-Powers' own homelands, i.e., what is sometimes referred to as "central strategic systems". In the "Memorandum of Understanding Regarding Establishment of a Data Base" the two countries for the first time have declared their possession of the following numbers of such strategic arms as at 18 June 1979:

	United States	USSR
Launchers of ICBMs	1,054	1,398
Fixed launchers of ICBMs	1,054	1,398
Launchers of ICBMs equipped with MIRVs	550	608
Launchers of SLBMs	656	950
Launchers of SLBMs equipped with MIRVs	496	144
Heavy bombers	573	156
Heavy bombers equipped for cruise missiles capable of range in excess of 600 km.	3	0
ASBMs (air-to-surface ballistic missiles)	0	0

Of the 1,054 missile launchers in the United States ICBM force, 550 have MIRVed Minuteman-III missiles with three warheads, each of 170 kt. yield. The remaining ICBMs are all single-warhead type, 450 of which are the Minuteman II, having a yield of 1-2 Mt., and 54 Titan II, with a 5-10 Mt. warheads.

The Minuteman III is the most accurate missile in the United States arsenal, with a CEP reported to be better than 300 m. With the installation of a new warhead of 350 kt. yield in 300 of the Minuteman III, as well as completed guidance improvements, the missile will have a higher probability to destroy an adversary's hardened silos, although it is stated that this probability would still be "modest".

On the Soviet side there are many classes of ICBMs deployed as shown in appendix III, with up to 8 warheads of 500 kt. each, deployed on the MIRVed SS-18 mod. 2.⁶ The largest deployed warhead is on the single-warhead SS-18 and has a yield of about 20 Mt. The CEP of the SS-18 is believed to be about equal to that of the Minuteman III.

For a number of years the United States has had 41 SLBM-equipped submarines, with a total of 656 missiles. About 500 of these are MIRVed Poseidon missiles with an average of 10 warheads, each with a yield of 40 kt. The remaining somewhat older missiles are of the multiple warhead type, but are not independently targetable. This means that they would separate in flight and have different impact points, which, however, cannot be pre-selected according to their strategic value. Each of these warheads has a yield of 200 kt., with a missile range of 4,000 to 5,000 km.

The new Trident submarine will first be deployed late in 1980 or early in 1981 with the Trident I (also denoted Trident C-4) MIRVed missile of more than 7,000 km. range, which will also have been substituted in the Poseidon submarines. This Trident submarine will carry 24 MIRVed missiles, be quieter and faster, and will have an expanded operating area. At the same time, it needs less operating area to remain within range of its targets.

Most Soviet deployed SLBMs are presently non-MIRVed, except for the SS-N-18 which has 3 warheads of about 200 kt. yield and a range believed to be similar to that of Trident. Soviet missile-launching submarines equipped with these missiles have a vastly expanded operating area and are less vulnerable to anti-submarine warfare.

On the United States side, the bomber force contains 300 to 350 B-52 long-range bombers. The United States bomber force is kept at a high level of ground alert, as it is vulnerable to SLBM attack, of which only a few minutes' warning would be available. The two Soviet corresponding types of long-range bombers are the Tupolev 95 and the Myasishchev, known in the West as the Bear and the Bison, respectively. There are about 150 of these aircraft.

According to the official United States Department of Defense estimates, independently targetable weapons in ICBMs, SLBMs and long-range bombers add up to over 9,000 for the United States side and about 6,000 for the Soviet Union. (The total numbers of weapons in the strategic stockpiles could be considerably larger, as is indicated in table 1 on page 27. These numbers are expected to increase in the next few years by at least 40 per cent with continued MIRVing, introduction of new cruise missiles and the deployment of the Trident submarine.

The power and number of these strategic weapons is difficult to grasp. Consider that a single Poseidon submarine with its 16 MIRVed missiles can deliver warheads to 160 separate targets; these warheads have a total explosive yield of 6.4 Mt., a larger explosive power than that of all the munitions fired in the Second World War; still, this megatonnage is of the order of one or a few thousandths of the megatonnage in either the United States or the Soviet strategic arsenal.

Regional nuclear forces (nuclear weapons of medium or intermediate range)

In addition to these central strategic forces, both super-Powers have many weapon systems with somewhat shorter ranges. These systems (and similar weapons belonging to other nuclear-weapon States) are sometimes referred to as "grey area" weapons or, in a European context, as "Eurostrategic" weapons. If the word "strategic" is used in its ordinary military sense, then indeed most nuclear weapons can be used for strategic purposes. If "grey area" weapons are sometimes thought of as a special category, it is mainly because they could reach not only targets in countries other than those of the super-Powers but also, by forward deployment, targets on the territories of the super-Powers themselves.

There is no clear borderline between these weapons and, for

instance, the SLBM forces already described. It is common practice, however, to single out medium-range (800-2,400 km.) ballistic missiles (MRBM), intermediate-range (2,400-6,400 km.) ballistic missiles (IRBM) and medium-range bomber aircraft as particularly important for non-central strategic employment.

The Soviet Union has some 700 MRBMs and IRBMs deployed both in the western USSR and east of the Urals. Among them is the new, mobile SS-20 missile with a 3-MIRV payload. It is believed that over 100 of these have been deployed so far. Also the USSR possesses about 500 medium-range bombers, e.g., of the types Tu-16 "Badger" and Tu-22M "Backfire", capable of nuclear delivery. On the United States side there are 65 FB-111A medium-range bombers and 300-400 forward based short-range, nuclear capable strike aircraft of types F-4, F-111 and others. The United States arsenal has no IRBMs.

Strategic arsenals of other countries

Britain has 4 nuclear ballistic missile submarines, each with 16 Polaris A-3 missiles (3x200 kt., not independently targetable), with an operational radius of about 3,000 km. The Vulcan bomber fleet, formerly considered as a strategic nuclear component, is no longer listed as such in available sources. It has been reported recently that the British Government has decided to buy the American Trident C-4 submarine-launched ballistic missile, which will be equipped with British "Chevaline" warheads.

France possesses at present 64 SLBMs in 4 nuclear-powered submarines, 18 IRBMs and 6 squadrons of some 30 Mirage-IVA medium-range bombers. A fifth SLBM submarine is scheduled to be operational before 1985. The SLBMs have about a 5,000 km. range and 1 Mt. single warheads, the IRBMs, a range of some 3,000 km. and single warheads of 150 kt. yield.

China is estimated to have deployed 50 to 70 intermediate range ballistic missiles, 40 to 50 medium-range ballistic missiles, and two limited-range ICBMs. A flight test of a Chinese ICBM was conducted in the middle of May 1980. Also in China's strategic force are Tu-16 and Tu-4 medium-range bombers. China's stockpile of weapons, fission and fusion, probably amounts to 225-300 with fission warhead yields in the 20-40 kt. range and fusion warheads of 3-4 Mt.

Tactical nuclear forces

Tactical nuclear weapons are common terms for those nuclear weapons systems which, by virtue of their range and yield as well as the way they are incorporated in a military organization, have been designed or can be used for employment against military targets in a theatre of war.[7] Such weapons are artillery shells, ground mobile rockets and missiles, air-launched bombs, rockets and missiles (with aircraft operating from carriers as well as land bases) and atomic demolition munitions ("land mines"). Naval forces of this kind comprise submarine-launched cruise or ballistic missiles, torpedoes and short-range, submarine-launched anti-submarine warfare rockets. Ground-based systems have ranges from about 15 km. (artillery) to several hundreds of km. (heavy missiles). Yield may vary from less than 0.1 to more than 100 kt.

As for short-range (under 800 km.) ballistic missiles (SRBM), the United States has deployed in Europe some 108 Pershing in the high-kiloton range and some 36 Lance in the low-kiloton range, while the Soviet Union has some 1,300 "Frog" 7, SS-1b, SS-1c, SS-12 and SS-21, some of which are believed to have megaton-yield warheads. France has a tactical nuclear force equipped with 32 short-range (about 120 km.) ballistic missiles called Pluton. These are believed to have about 20 kt. warheads.

Some of the non-nuclear-weapon States which are members of NATO, as well as Warsaw Pact States other than the Soviet Union, have in their armed forces short-range ballistic missiles which are capable of nuclear delivery. These are some 200 Pershing, Honest John and Lance missiles on the NATO side and about 330 SS-1b, SS-1c and "Frog" 7 missiles on the Warsaw Pact side. However, all nuclear warheads for these missiles are in United States and Soviet custody, respectively.

Aside from the strategic submarine-launched missiles already

mentioned, the Soviet Union has about 80 older short-range ballistic missiles (SS-N-4 and SS-N-5, with warheads of megaton
yield) based on submarines. There are also one or a few hundred
sea-launched aerodynamic missiles (SS-N-3, with a kiloton yield
warhead) deployed on cruisers and submarines. No other State is
known to possess this type of system.

The United States has some 1,000 aerodynamic air-launched
missiles of short range with warheads of 100 to 200 kiloton yield.
These are denoted SRAMs (short-range attack missiles). On the
Soviet side, approximately the same number of AS-3 "Kanga-
roo", AS-4 "Kitchen" and AS-6 "Kingfish" missiles of kiloton
yield have long been available, probably for use against surface
ships.

In addition to the medium-range bombers already enumerated,
there are many types of aircraft in many nations which are or
could be made nuclear-capable for short-range missions. The
land-based strike aircraft of the United States deployed in Europe
comprise 300 to 400 nuclear-capable aircraft, where the Soviet
Union has about 1,000. The United States also possesses 100 to
200 carrier-based strike aircraft capable of delivering nuclear
weapons against targets on sea or land. It is not clear how many of
the large force of F-104 and F-4 in the other NATO States or Su-7
and Su-20 on the Warsaw Pact side actually have a nuclear role.

In principle, artillery pieces of 155 mm. calibre or larger are
nuclear-capable. Both the Soviet Union and the United States
have in their regular army units several hundred such artillery
pieces, as they are primarily intended to fire conventional shells.
Nuclear artillery shells for 155 mm. and 203 mm. pieces have
been developed in the United States and are also deployed in
Europe. They are generally believed to have yields from a fraction of a kiloton up to a few kilotons. Some sources state without
qualification that the Soviet Union also has these nuclear munitions.

Atomic demolition munitions (ADMs) are designed to function somewhat like conventional land mines, creating craters and
other obstacles to an advancing enemy. Only the United States is

known to have manufactured this type of nuclear explosive, but any nuclear charge of suitable size could probably be quickly adapted for the purpose. No emplacement is known to have taken place.

Very few data are available on some naval nuclear-weapon systems, which have for many years been said to exist at least in the United States arsenal. Most frequently mentioned are the American ASROC and SUBROC ASW rocket-torpedoes with an alleged yield of 1 kt.[8] Reportedly, there are also nuclear depth-charges with 5 to 10 kt. yield. Whether or not nuclear sea mines are at present available anywhere is unclear.

Europe is a zone of very high concentration of tactical nuclear weapons. An often quoted figure is that the United States disposes of about 7,000 such weapons in Europe, in many depots in the territories of several countries. The Soviet Union is believed to possess more than 3,000 weapons of this kind for use in Europe.

Techniques and costs of acquiring nuclear weapons

The previous United Nations study on nuclear weapons contained an analysis of the cost of the acquisition and further development of these weapons. Since then some further studies which provide data about the availability of nuclear technology have become available, notably from the International Conference on Nuclear Power and Its Fuel Cycle held at Salzburg, Austria, under the auspices of the International Atomic Energy Agency (1977) and the International Fuel Cycle Evaluation (INFCE, 1980). These studies have been utilized to update the previous analyses.[9]

To be a nuclear-weapon State, a nation must necessarily possess an explosive device based on the nuclear fission of either uranium or plutonium. Uranium, as found in nature, is a mixture of several isotopes which differ by only about 1 per cent in weight, but greatly in nuclear properties. The fissile isotope uranium-235 forms only 0.7 per cent of natural uranium, the rest being uranium-238. Uranium-238 is fissile only by very high-energy neutrons and cannot be used to make a fission weapon. The uranium-235 fraction must therefore be increased in an isotope enrichment facility to in principle more than 5 per cent, in practice say 20 per cent or more. For technical and economical reasons, the "weapon-grade" uranium used in nuclear weapons will contain 90-95 per cent uranium-235. This enrichment process is very expensive and requires advanced technology. As an example of the cost, the three United States separation plants (based on gaseous diffusion) required an investment cost of about $4,500 million (in 1980 dollars). Annual maintenance and operation costs are estimated at $500 to 600 million. These United States plants could produce about 100,000 kg. of 90 per cent uranium-235 annually, enough for some 4,000 fission weapons. It should be noted that these plants also enrich uranium for civil purposes. Enrichment plants of comparable size exist in the Soviet Union and smaller plants have been built in France, the United Kingdom and China. A large plant is presently under construction in France with the participation of Belgium, Italy and Spain for the production of low-enriched uranium for peaceful use in power-producing reactors.

Uranium-235 can also be enriched by aerodynamic processes, most importantly by centrifugation. The production of a few weapons per year would require a centrifuge enrichment plant with an investment cost of about $50 million. The construction time could be estimated as about 5 to 7 years, for a State with no previous experience with this technology. A larger plant, giving material sufficient for 200 weapons annually, would require an investment of about $500 million and 6 or 7 years construction time for an industrialized nation. Operation and maintenance costs as a percentage of capital costs are in the 25 to 30 per cent range. Centrifuge enrichment plants are known to exist or to be under construction in the United States, the Soviet Union, the United Kingdom, Japan and the Netherlands. The plant in the Netherlands is a joint project between several European countries, including the United Kingdom and the Federal Republic of Germany. A pilot plant based on a different aerodynamic concept, the vortex tube, exists in South Africa. Among non-aerodynamic methods, laser enrichment is attracting increasing interest.

Plutonium-239 is normally produced in a nuclear reactor. A production line for plutonium requires the capability to refine uranium, the fabrication of reactor fuel, a nuclear reactor and a chemical plant for plutonium extraction from the spent fuel elements (reprocessing).

It is easier to construct and operate a dedicated plutonium production reactor than an electrical power producing reactor. Investment costs for the simplest type of graphite moderated reactor giving enough plutonium-239 for one or two weapons annually (10 kg. plutonium) are estimated to be in the range of $13 to 26 million (1976 dollars). The capital cost of a reprocessing plant to extract plutonium from the irradiated fuel would amount to an additional $25 million (1976 dollars). Personnel requirements for construction and operation are modest and plutonium could be produced 4 years after the start of the construction. In order to obtain plutonium for 10 to 20 weapons per year with a safe and reliable reactor, investment costs would range from $250 to 500 million and require some 50 to 75 engineers and 150 to 200 skilled technicians. The time span until the first output of plutonium would be 5 to 7 years.

According to some estimates, the total amount worldwide of weapon-grade uranium produced since the Second World War ranges between 1,000 and 2,000 tons. Similarly, the total quantity of weapon-grade plutonium produced worldwide amounts to 100-200 tons.

A problem of growing concern has been the possibility of using plutonium produced in ordinary nuclear-power reactors as the explosive material in atomic bombs. The core of the matter is the presence of other plutonium isotopes, particularly plutonium-240, which increase in abundance with the time of exposure in the reactor. While it is clear that so-called reactor-grade plutonium, i.e., with a concentration of plutonium-240 higher than, say, 10 per cent, might be used to produce a nuclear explosive, it is also clear that such an explosive is more difficult to design and fabricate, and will generally have a very low yield which cannot be predicted with the accuracy possible if weapon-grade plutonium had been used. It would thus be considered less suitable to use reactor-grade plutonium in military nuclear weapons, while a device based on such plutonium could still be very destructive.

It should be pointed out in this connexion that it might be possible to manipulate the operation of some power reactors to produce weapon-grade plutonium, even if a country contemplating the manufacture of nuclear weapons might prefer, for reasons of cost and operational simplicity, to install separate reactors for production of weapon-grade plutonium. It should also be pointed out that some research reactors do produce small but significant quantities of weapon-grade plutonium, and that some others are fuelled with weapon-grade uranium. Finally, it should be noted that it is not possible to make a weapon out of the uranium content of commercial light-water reactor fuel, as this contains only 3 per cent of the isotope uranium-235 and thus can never attain a fast critical mass.

Uranium-233, which can be produced by irradiating thorium with neutrons, is a third fissile isotope theoretically suitable for fission weapons. No weapons are known to have been constructed from uranium-233, however, partly due to gamma radiation hazards of material containing uranium-233.

For the production of nuclear weapons there are further expenses of warhead-assembly and weapon-testing. The previous United Nations study estimated that a plutonium-weapon programme that produced ten 20 kt. devices over ten years would cost around $200 million or $20 million per warhead. A programme that produced 100 such warheads would cost $375 million or about $3.8 million per warhead.

The costs connected with an advanced delivery system for the weapon are typically in the range of many thousands of millions of dollars. There is a need for ensuring the reliability of the delivery vehicles and their protection against attack, which can add substantially to the cost. On the other hand, simpler and cheaper solutions might be considered by a State contemplating the buildup of a small, perhaps secret, nuclear-weapon capability. Because of the evolution of technology, including nuclear power, electronics, chemical engineering and the like, the real cost of developing nuclear weapons is now less than it was in 1945.

Table 1. Rough estimates of current nuclear arsenals[a]
(Total number of warheads and total yield in Mt.)

Nation	"Central strategic"		Other systems		Total[b]	
	Warheads[c]	Mt[d]	Warheads[d]	Mt[d]	Warheads	Mt
United States of America	9 000—11 000	3 000—4 000	16 000—22 000	1 000—4 000	25 000—33 000	4 000— 8 000
USSR	6 000— 7 500	5 000—8 000	5 000— 8 000	2 000—3 000	11 000—15 000	7 000—11 000
United Kingdom			200— 1 000		200— 1 000	200— 1 000
China					<300	200— 400
France					<200	<100
Rounded grand total					37 000—50 000	11 000—20 000

a. These estimates were made for this report by the Swedish National Defence Research Institute in co-operation with the Institute for Defense and Disarmament Studies, Brookline, Mass. They are based on available open sources. Among these are *SIPRI Yearbook 1980* as well as *The Military Balance, 1979–1980*. As is apparent from the table, there are substantial uncertainties in all the estimates. The largest single source of uncertainty is lack of knowledge regarding numbers and powers of weapons for aircraft delivery. In addition, some of these weapons are believed to have variable yields. Other uncertainties are introduced by the fact that different sources refer to different times, by differing assumptions as to the state of various systems under conversion, etc. Multiple re-entry vehicles have been counted separately, and assumptions have been made regarding possible reserves of certain weapons. It should be noted that calculations based on estimates of the amount of fissile material that could have been produced might lead to considerably higher figures for the possible number of warheads.

b. Figures for the two super-Powers are rounded to the nearest thousands, for other nations to the nearest hundreds.

c. Figures rounded to the nearest five hundreds.

d. Figures rounded to the nearest thousands.

III

Trends in the Technological Development of Nuclear-Weapon Systems [10]

Main features of past and present development

THE ONGOING TECHNOLOGICAL DEVELOPMENT of nuclear-weapon systems is sometimes described as necessitated by threats to national security, and as a corollary to the evolution of theories or doctrines for the use of nuclear weapons. It is widely believed, however, that new weapon systems emerge not because of any military or security considerations but because technology by its own impetus often takes the lead over policy, creating weapons for which needs have to be invented and deployment theories have to be readjusted. It is also a fact that a very substantial portion of the world's total scientific and technical manpower is engaged in military research and development, involving the improvement of existing weapons and developing new weapon systems. It is obvious that a situation involving an effort of this magnitude must lead to the production of new and more destructive weapons. One should also keep in mind that the long lead-time required for the development of new nuclear-weapon systems does bring in significant qualitative changes to the action/reaction process since one side, wishing to catch up with the other side, has necessarily to take into account possible future developments by the other side over significantly long time frames.

In the 1950s and early 1960s, the nuclear arms race was characterized by the development of ever more powerful weapons. The first fusion device detonated by the United States in 1952 had a yield reported to be about 10 Mt. Two years later the United States tested a weapon with a 15 Mt. yield, and in 1961 the USSR exploded a fusion weapon with an estimated yield of about 60 Mt. In later years, the trend has been towards smaller but more numerous weapons. On an individual missile, for instance, a single large warhead may be replaced by several smaller ones of the same total weight; in many cases this leads to a decrease in the total nominal yield although the number of warheads increases. Thus the 20 Mt. warhead of the Soviet SS-18 missile can be replaced by an alternative payload containing 10 warheads of about 500 kt. Similarly, the air-launched cruise missiles which the United States will have well under deployment by 1982 have yields in the range below 200 kt., considerably less than the gravity bomb which they replace in the penetrating bomber force.

As was shown in chapter II, the lethality of the weapons increases although the nominal yield may decrease, as this trend in warhead development has been accompanied by an increase in the accuracy of the delivery vehicles. The momentum that this enhancement of delivery accuracy is giving to the strategic nuclear arms race can hardly be exaggerated. By opening to each super-Power the possibility of hitting the other's nuclear-weapon emplacements, it creates a situation of a "duel" between the strategic weapons and gives fresh nourishment to the fears that the opponent might become able to make a disarming first strike. This threat was also the rationale for the introduction of SLBMs.

The development of large numbers of still more accurate nuclear weapons, even though their yields may be moderate, makes it increasingly more difficult to protect land-based nuclear weapons from an attack, i.e., a first strike aiming at eliminating these weapons. Even hardened silos may no longer provide sufficient protection. In consequence, military planners have been and are still searching for new countermethods or countersystems that would be safe from attack and maintain "a stable deterrence".

Figure III. The Trade-Off Between Weapon Yield and Delivery Accuracy

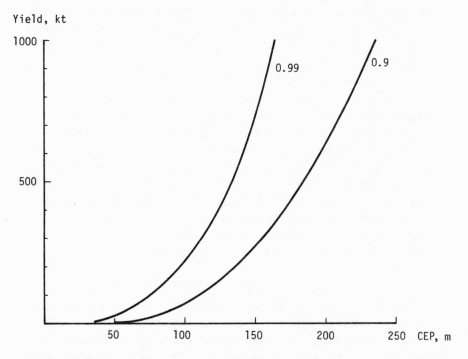

Yield, kt

When weapon delivery accuracy in enhanced, i.e., CEP is reduced, the weapon yield required to achieve a certain probability of destroying a given target decreases sharply. The diagram illustrates this relationship for probability values 0.99 and 0.9, assuming a target hardened to 10 MPa (100 atm or 1,450 PSI) to be destroyed by blast from an explosion close to the ground.

This also involves the further development of elaborate detection and identification systems in order to receive advance warning of an impending attack. This new aspect of the nuclear arms race will be described in more detail in the following paragraphs.

The arms control agreements concluded so far have not, in essence, significantly restricted this development. It is true that the SALT I agreement between the United States and the USSR succeeded in putting a narrow limit on the deployment of one particular type of countersystem, the so-called anti-ballistic missiles (ABMs). However, it offered no substantial constraints on the development of means already devised to penetrate or circumvent an ABM defence, notably the introduction of MIRVs. The possible importance in this respect of the SALT II treaty, when and if ratified, is treated below, and so are the implications of conceivable limitations on nuclear-weapon testing.

There is also an ongoing technical development in the field of theatre or tactical nuclear weapons, although it has hitherto attracted less public attention than that in the strategic weapons realm. The thrust of this development is, generally speaking, towards greater flexibility in handling and operation. As was indicated in chapter II, this has already led to the creation of a plethora of different weapon types, some multi-purpose, others intended for special objectives. This is also covered to some extent in what follows.

Warhead design and characteristics

The single most outstanding feature in warhead development up to now has been the reduction of size and weight in relation to yield. This process has made possible the design of multiple warheads on strategic missiles, as well as some of the weapons denoted as tactical.

The bombs that levelled Hiroshima and Nagasaki weighed about 5 tons each and could not have been delivered by any other carriers than heavy bombers. By comparison, the Poseidon submarine-launched missile, with a total throw-weight of 1,000 kg., carries 10 warheads, each of three times the yield of Hiroshima bomb. This represents a 150-fold increase in the yield-to-weight ratio.

Another example is given by the nuclear artillery shells mentioned in chapter II, which demonstrate that it is possible to build nuclear explosives so small that the outer diameter of the casing is 155 mm., and so light that the explosive, its associated safety, arming and firing mechanisms and the metal casing altogether do not weigh much more than 40 kg., which is the approximate weight of a conventional 155 mm. shell.

From available data on MIRVs and other devices, it seems likely that, at least in the United States, this "miniaturization" of nuclear warheads is now, in some applications, close to the limits set by the laws of physics. Other nuclear-weapon States may be approaching—or already have achieved—the same levels of compactness, but they may also put their priorities differently. As has been indicated earlier, the Soviet Union has developed MIRV technology.

Other warhead design improvements have concerned weapon safety, reliability, versatility and hardening against adverse environments. Safety measures aim at minimizing both the risk of accidents in handling the weapon and the possibility of unauthorized use. The weapon may include, for instance, a device which can be armed only upon receipt of a particular, coded radio signal. Reliability may be enhanced in many ways, from the choice of special materials to prevent deterioration of weapon components, to the particular designs needed to withstand the tremendous accelerations in a gun tube. Versatility could be enhanced by designing a warhead in such a way that different yields can be selected easily.

There is also an economic aspect of the technical development of warheads. If steps are taken to ensure the longest possible lifetime of a warhead, costly maintenance procedures or replacements can be postponed or perhaps abandoned. Where large numbers of weapons are involved, the associated maintenance costs are probably considerable.

Low-yield weapons around or below 1 kt. seem to have existed for a long time in the United States arsenal and to be deployed, for instance, in Europe. However, there exists the possibility of developing and deploying nuclear weapons with extremely low yields, down to a few tons equivalent of high explosive. Such "mini-nukes" could be delivered with sufficient accuracy to destroy small targets. They would, however, have no apparent benefit in reduced cost or a higher probability of destroying an intended target; they would be used rather to reduce the destruction from blast in the surroundings of the target. The limited radius for material damage raised the question of the possible "conventionalization" of the mini-nukes, i.e., whether they could be used without risk for further escalation. After some international debate, however, the USSR, the United Kingdom and the United States have declared that they would not for the time being deploy nuclear weapons with small yields in such a way as to blur the nuclear threshold.

The development of nuclear weapons continues at a very active pace. Recently, emphasis has been put not only on the manufacture of warheads with different yields, but also on changing other weapon characteristics. The proportion of energy that is derived from fission and fusion, respectively, can be varied within large limits. By surrounding a weapon with casings of various kinds, the radiation properties may be changed. While initial radiation will generally decrease with increasing mass of the weapon casing, residual radiation can be either increased or decreased.

The most widely discussed example is the so-called "neutron bomb", referred to as an "enhanced radiation" (ER) weapon in official United States sources. The neutron bomb, which is a relatively old concept, would be arranged so that a large amount of its explosive energy comes from the fusion of deuterium with tritium. While this reaction gives rise to more energetic neutrons than a fission chain reaction, the design of the weapon would be such as to minimize the conversion of neutron energy into blast and heat. For a hypothetical 1 kt. ER weapon, the zone of danger due to neutrons would considerably exceed that due to blast. This has been described as an advantage when the weapon is employed against armoured forces, as armoured vehicles are quite resistant to blast and heat but offer little shielding against neutrons. Consequently, these weapons would produce lethal doses of radiation to unprotected people at considerable distances, and many would be killed by radiation in regions in which structures, vehicles, etc., would be left intact by blast. The neutron bomb would be more costly to manufacture than would a 10 kt. weapon of the same radiation range and greater blast action. Both mini-nukes and neutron bombs can be seen as expressions of an effort to make nuclear weapons less destructive to the surroundings if they were to be used in actual warfare and thus, according to their proponents, make nuclear deterrence at the tactical level more credible.

Plans by the United States to produce the neutron weapon and to introduce it in Europe have been halted for the time being. The French Government has recently announced that France has developed and tested neutron bombs, and that decisions on production and deployment will be taken in the years to come. The Soviet leadership has stated that the Soviet Union has developed and tested a neutron bomb but decided not to deploy it at present.

Another type of "tailored-effects" weapon discussed in the United States is the "reduced residual-radiation" (RRR) or "minimum residual-radiation" (MRR) weapon. Like the ER weapon, this would derive a substantial part of its energy from fusion, but the weapon casing would be designed so as to reduce the outflux of neutrons. Such weapons, which could probably have a significantly larger yield than the proposed ER warheads, could be used in surface or subsurface burst; for instance to create huge craters with a significantly smaller amount of radioactive fallout than an ordinary fission warhead.

There has been a great deal of both speculation and serious research regarding the possibility of building a thermonuclear explosive without a fission explosion as initiator. In particular, the use of lasers to initiate fusion reactions has been studied. However, there appears to be no prospect for success along these lines, in anything that might be used as a deliverable nuclear weapon.

Despite the research and development going on in the field of special types of warheads, no major breakthrough is likely to occur with regard to the basic design principles of nuclear explosives. The evolution of delivery systems seems likely to carry more practical importance in the future, as it has already done for some years.

Nuclear testing

A most crucial question is what influence nuclear-weapon tests may have on the future development of warheads, as the answer is of central importance to the efforts to achieve a comprehensive test ban. The nuclear test activity is still considerable. Since the first nuclear explosion in 1945 the nuclear Powers have performed more than 1,200 nuclear tests. The exact number is not officially known, but some more detailed figures are given in chapter IV.

According to American sources,[11] United States tests during the late 1970s were conducted for the following main purposes:

(a) Improvement of yield-to-weight ratios;

(b) Reduction of warhead cost and special nuclear material and consumption;

(c) Enhancement of warhead safety;

(d) Increase of weapon control to prevent unauthorized use;

(e) Tailoring of weapons effects to specific military needs;

(f) Understanding of long-term chemical and structural stability.

This reflects the technological trends described above. The list contains the purposes for advanced development and testing stated to be important in view of the possibility of a comprehensive test ban. A major purpose for testing is normally the requirements caused by adaptation of warheads to new or modified weapon systems or vehicles.

The distribution, by percentage, of tests made in the United States from the end of 1963 to 1971 (excluding 21 "Plowshare" tests for civil objectives) has been presented[12] as follows:

65 per cent—Weapon development tests

16 per cent—Validation tests

 9 per cent—Weapons effects tests

 5 per cent—Combined weapon development and validation tests

 5 per cent—Combined weapon effects and validation tests

By "validation" is meant essentially the final confirmation, if required, of the functioning of a completed weapon, while "development" refers to the earlier, more explorative design stages. It should be noted that "stockpile testing", i.e., sampling to check the function of stockpiled weapons, is not mentioned. There are indications, however, that at least the United States has made very few tests with the sole purpose of checking the stockpile.

Those favouring a comprehensive test ban claim that it will impede the evolution of nuclear-weapon technology among the existing nuclear Powers, contribute to prevent the proliferation of nuclear weapons among nations which do not now possess them and generally de-emphasize nuclear weaponry.

Those opposing a comprehensive test ban argue that nuclear stockpiles would become less reliable, and that one would have to forgo nuclear-weapon developments leading to nuclear weapons which are safer against accident and more controllable. The view is also expressed that the nuclear-weapon Powers would need to continue to test in order to stay ahead of those nuclear Powers that have not signed the partial test-ban treaty.

It might be technically possible for a nuclear-weapon Power to maintain a stockpile (without improving it) by non-nuclear testing and remanufacture of components which age, corrode or otherwise become unacceptable for use in the stockpile. Still, as long as nuclear weapons exist, there would be pressures for changes in the stockpiles that may require nuclear-weapon testing.

From the discussion above, one may conclude that a comprehensive test ban would make more difficult the continued development of sophisticated weapons within the established nuclear powers and thus have an inhibiting effect on the arms race. A comprehensive test ban would also have value in preventing horizontal proliferation: it would, in particular, reinforce the political commitment to non-proliferation undertaken by States Parties to the Treaty on the Non-Proliferation of Nuclear Weapons. It may be technically possible for many States to develop unsophisticated fission weapons and to have some confidence in their reliability, without carrying out a test. It is unlikely, however, that States would wish to commit their national security for any length of time to nuclear-weapon systems that are untested. Development of advanced systems such as thermo-nuclear weapons or systems with strict military specifications would be, according to accepted engineering common sense, very uncertain if testing was not possible. Part of the test-ban discussion has focused on lowering the present threshold of 150 kt., which does not seem to have had any strong attenuating influence on the technological development of nuclear weapons.

General comments on weapon systems

Any modern weapon system consists of several major components in addition to the warhead. Such components are the vehicle (e.g., a missile) which carries the warhead to the target; the platform (e.g., a submarine or a silo) from which the vehicle is launched; the command, control and communications equipment by which the system is activated and, in some cases, directed; and the particular means of intelligence that give the signal for its activation. All or some of these components may be very closely adapted to each other, but some may have a multiple function, connecting with several systems.

There is a continuous evolution of all these components—and their subcomponents—which is too complex to explore in all its possible combinations. Different basic principles may be exploited for similar purposes, by themselves or in conjunction. Different technical solutions for particular components may be combined in a multitude of ways. And, perhaps most important, each new step may give rise to several potential countermea-

Figure IV. Effect of Mirving

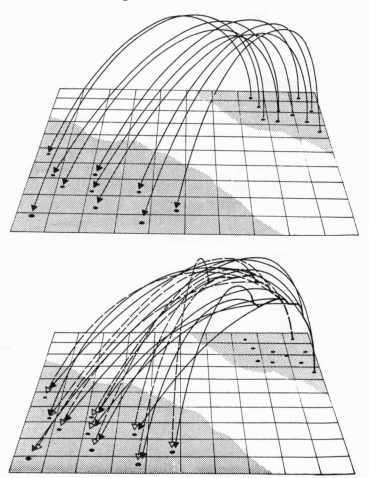

Before the advent of MIRVed missiles a preemptive attack by one country's ICBM force against the other country's ICBM force would have required the expenditure of at least one of the attacking country's missiles for each of the attacked country's missile silos (top). With a MIRVed missile force, however, one country could in principle devote only a fraction of its missiles to an attack against the other's missiles, expecting to destroy most if not all of them while retaining most of its own missiles safe in their silos (bottom). In this case it is conceivable some advantage could be gained by attacking first. Attacking MIRVs are shown cross-targeted, two to a silo. (*Scientific American*, Nov. 1979)

sures, which in turn may call for various counter-countermeasures; thus the possibilities multiply to defy comprehensive descriptions.

Guidance systems for vehicles (and for some types of mobile platforms) are of particular interest. Here it is necessary to distinguish between ballistic missiles, which are guided mainly during the "boosting" phase, i.e., the initial part of the flight when the rocket engines work; vehicles like cruise missiles, which are driven through the entire flight path and for which guidance becomes navigation; and weapons (of any kind) in their final approach to the target, when target-finding and homing devices developed for conventional munitions might be used.

To improve long-range navigation, the inertial guidance systems which have long been used need to be supplemented by intermittent, precise position information. This can be provided by a set of satellites in geostationary orbit as illustrated, e.g., by the United States Global Positioning System (GPS) or Navigation System using Time And Range (NAVSTAR). For cruise missiles and other low-flying vehicles, it is possible to scan the ground below and compare the results with data filed in the computer memory of the vehicle. This could be done by measuring only the vertical profile of the ground (e.g., Terrain Contour Matching or TERCOM) or by scanning some of its area properties (e.g., Map Matching or MM). Of these techniques, GPS or NAV-STAR is said to have been established but not deployed, and there are reports of some technical difficulties regarding actual deployment. TERCOM is well advanced and MM still experimental.

For homing a weapon on the target, a number of sensors have been developed to govern the operations of steering mechanisms in the projectile. These homing systems include a variety of radar, infrared and laser devices. Some of them could be adapted for use within strategic vehicles; others may be used to enhance the accuracy of various tactical nuclear weapons. To what extent the nuclear-weapon States have already implemented such options is not known, although nuclear-weapon States have not deployed guidance systems for re-entry vehicles from ballistic missiles.

Advances in propulsion technology are also highly relevant for the evolution of nuclear forces, the most recent example being the development of the cruise missile. Jet-propelled, aerodynamic missiles were first introduced in the Second World War and have since been deployed in many types (with conventional warheads) by many nations. However, the development in later years of extremely light-weight, highly efficient jet engines in conjunction with advanced navigation systems and nuclear warheads has moved the cruise missile into the strategic area, while at the same time adding to its importance as a theatre weapon.

Various facilities of command, control and communication are supposed to be used by the nuclear-weapon States to satisfy the two requirements: not to allow an unauthorized launch of nuclear weapons and to permit the command authority to release nuclear weapons when it has been so decided. The command, control and communication system which is designed for these purposes may not, however, have the capability to provide for various levels of retaliation with nuclear weapons. This would pose very serious problems, which would need to be solved in a time of ultimate confusion and massive destruction. These problems are particularly troublesome in the case of nuclear weapons which are far away in submarines, as it is required that these weapons be in instant readiness. In this context it should be remembered that intercontinental missiles arrive at their targets in 30 minutes whereas short-range ballistic missiles arrive in a still shorter time, 5 to 7 minutes. For these reasons, the techniques of rapid detection and identification are an important part of the technological race between the super-Powers. Of special interest in this context are the space-based systems.

Numerous satellites also exist which are important in communication, navigation and particularly in the monitoring of international agreements. The latter, as defined in the SALT I and SALT II agreements, are given special status by the signatories and are protected against interference. However, many useful satellites have no role in the monitoring of SALT provisions and are therefore not specifically guaranteed against interference or even harm.

Strategic delivery systems

The evolution of guidance systems has brought ICBMs from an accuracy of several kilometres in the 1950s to a stated accuracy of the order of 200 m. (0.1 mmi) now. The provision of robust radio guidance to the missiles during boost (or terminal guidance) would allow accuracies to be improved considerably over the present 200 m. limit, perhaps down to the range of 50 m. CEP. ICBMs have also evolved in readiness and controllability from the cryogenically fuelled missiles, which could with difficulty be fired on 10-minute notice, to storable-liquid or solid-fuel missiles, which can be launched within a few seconds after receipt of an order.

The most recently discussed ICBM is the mobile MX missile. In June 1979, the President of the United States authorized the full-scale development of this missile, to carry 10 MIRVed warheads with a sub-megaton yield and a range of 11,000 km. The key aspect of this missile is that it would be encapsulated, with missile and capsule weighing together about 175 tons. A "race-track" basing-mode for the MX was later selected. In this system, 200 "race tracks" of about 45 km. circumference would each be equipped with 23 shelters and one MX missile along with a transporter-erector-launcher (TEL). A "shield vehicle" would visit each of the 23 shelters in turn. The shield vehicle would contain either the missile and its TEL or a simulator (or decoy), so that even close observation would not enable one to determine which shelter contained the missile. Furthermore, the automated TEL would have the ability to move on warning, so that if information of an ICBM launch against the MX complex was obtained, some or all of the 200 TEL would dash from the shelters in which they had been hidden and secrete the MX in another shelter.

Estimates of the required expenditure for this system range from some $30,000 million to $60,000 million or more, of which only about $3,000 million is for the procurement of the missiles

Figure V. Actual and Possible Future Development of Missile Accuracy

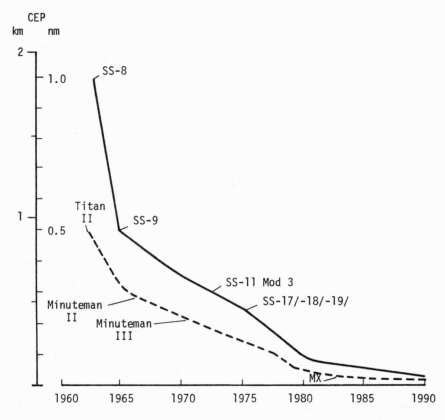

Estimated development of ICBM accuracy 1960-90. (From Gray, Colin S., *The Future of Land-Based Missile Forces*, Adelphi Paper No. 140, International Institute of Strategic Studies, London, 1978.) It should be noted that the estimates described by the graph are projections made in 1977 and that the curves do not necessarily reflect the actual development after that year.

themselves. It has been observed that a system in which the basing mode costs $30,000 million or more, while the procurement of
missiles costs "only" $3,000 million, may encourage the possi-
bility of multiplying the number of missiles in the hardened basing system by a factor of 8 for perhaps only a 50 per cent increase
in over-all system cost. A super-Power contemplating such a basing mode could be said to instil in its adversary (and in the nations
of the world) the expectation that, at some time, very much larger
numbers of missiles and nuclear warheads would be deployed
than were originally announced as the plan for the system. For
this reason, means to allow verification of the existing number of
missiles within the system are reportedly to be introduced.

The Soviet ICBM development up to now has been characterized by the introduction, in rapid succession, of many new
missile types while still retaining most of the older ones. Virtually all of the latter are believed to have megaton or multi-
megaton yield warheads, while those more recently deployed,
with an estimated CEP of 300-400 m., are reported to have up to
eight RVs, each with a yield in the high kiloton range. It would
thus appear that the over-all Soviet trend in improving the capability is similar to that in the United States, although the throw-
weight advantage of the USSR over the United States seems to
continue.

The present trends in the evolution of SLBM forces are not
only towards new missiles with more RVs and higher accuracy—
partly as a result of improved submarine navigation systems—but
also towards modernization of the submarines to acquire greater
quietness and expanded operational range. The United States is
beginning the deployment of the Trident I missile. With a range
of over 7,000 km. and a greater throw weight than the Poseidon
missile, it will replace this missile in the 31 Poseidon submarines.
It will also be deployed in some 10 24-tube Trident submarines
when these become operational. The United Kingdom is contemplating the acquisition of Trident I missiles and modern nuclear-
propelled submarines for the replacement of its 4-submarine
Polaris fleet. France is building a fifth SLBM submarine, pre-

sumably similar to the four already existing. Programmes for the technical development of Soviet SLBM forces are not well known; several new missiles have been introduced since the previous United Nations report, however. Among these are some 64 SS-N missiles (Soviet designator RSM-50) with 3 MIRVs of approximately 200 kt. yield.

Manoeuvring re-entry vehicles (MaRV) have been discussed since before the SALT I Treaty. The necessary technology is probably available, although no deployment is known so far. MaRVs were originally conceived as an aid for penetrating an ABM defence. With ABMs abolished by treaty, MaRVs are still being discussed to improve accuracy against a fixed target, to attack a target in motion, such as a ship or an aircraft, or to evade another type of defence.

In addition to MaRV, other penetration aids are possible. They include considerably improved hardening of the nuclear weapon or the RV itself and the potential deployment of decoys which resemble the real RVs in radar or infrared properties. One example of protecting re-entry vehicles in space against radar observation is to enclose each in an inflated aluminized balloon, so that similar balloons (empty) could serve as decoys.

The primary development in the delivery of nuclear weapons by aircraft concerns the planned long-range, air-launched cruise missiles (ALCM). Thus, the United States has a programme to introduce ALCMs of 2,400 km. range on its B-52 bombers in 1982, and to deploy some 3,000 with a warhead yield in the 200 kt. range. Because the ALCM is so much smaller than the aircraft itself, it would be more difficult to detect by radar, infrared radiation or other means; its smaller size would also make it less vulnerable to defensive measures such as guns, anti-aircraft missiles and the like. Its ability to fly at very low altitudes would add to the difficulties of detecting and engaging it. Finally, the fact that defensive systems would have to destroy 20 ALCMs rather than one penetrating bomber would require vastly more surface-to-air missiles and put a greater strain on the air defences than would an improved bomber aircraft.

The SALT II treaty between the United States and the USSR (cf. also chapter VII) would set nearly equal numerical limits on offensive systems that either country may deploy. The treaty would also have some impact on the further technological development of weapons, as it would limit re-entry vehicles on ICBMs, SLBMs and ASBMs to that number for which the missile had been tested. This is considered to be an important provision in the treaty as it sets a limit on the further "vertical" proliferation of nuclear warheads. In addition, the treaty would ban new heavy ICBMs and otherwise limit qualitative improvements on ICBMs, permitting the flight testing and deployment of only one new type of light ICBM on each side. There would be no restrictions on qualitative improvements on SLBMs, however.

In order to comply with the aggregate limits, the Soviet Union would have to dismantle 254 strategic delivery systems. The United States is at present within the final SALT II limits. Nevertheless, modernization programmes on both sides are continuing. The treaty would limit the Soviet forces to 6,200 ICBM warheads and 2,000 to 3,000 SLBM warheads in 1985, at which time the United States would have some 2,100 warheads on ICBMs, 6,300 on SLBMs and perhaps 3,000 on air-launched cruise missiles.

At present, the direction of the long-term evolution of the strategic forces is not at all clear. As one example of this, some experts argue that the technical facts which drove the super-Powers to prefer large submarines may now have changed. Designs are available for missiles which do not require maintenance from one year to the next. Furthermore, the deployment of satellite navigation systems and their possible coupling to the guidance computers of the missiles themselves means that even small missiles (which could not afford heavy guidance systems) may be highly accurate, and that their inertial guidance systems need not be so expensive as formerly. To take advantage of these developments, some advocate the introduction of small submarines, each carrying 2 or 4 missiles in hermetically-sealed capsules, outside the pressure hull of the submarine.

Strategic countermeasures and countersystems

The most direct way to attempt to negate the threat against strategic weapons would be to introduce a passive defence in the form of hardening. The missile silos in the Soviet Union and the United States have successively been hardened to levels estimated to be above 100 atmospheres, which is presumably close to the practical limit for these installations. Certain command and control posts may have hardness in the 200 atmosphere (almost 3,000 PSI) range. However, any such installation would be vulnerable to a direct hit unless it was so deep that the disturbance from a crater immediately above would not provide enough ground motion or faulting to damage the installation. Depths of the order of 2 km. are probably required, but no installations or plans are known which utilize such super-hardening.

To nullify or substantially invalidate the nuclear threat against civilian targets by the provision of adequate shelters for the population and the hardening of industrial structures is in practice impossible. This problem is more fully treated in chapter IV.

The problem of active defence against nuclear weapons primarily devolves upon the detection of such weapons, their location to an accuracy which allows a defending weapon to be directed against the attacking weapon, and the provision of adequate numbers of defending weapons to handle an attack.

The principal technique to counter these developments is to make systems mobile. This can be expected to be a major aspect in development of ballistic missile systems in the future.

As has been indicated earlier, the SALT I Treaty between the United States and the USSR effectively bans, indefinitely, the extensive deployment of an antiballistic missile system. In addition, it specifically bans mobile ABM, including those deployed in space.

On the other hand, the technical factors involved have in many cases combined to make the use of nuclear weapons for defence less effective than the use of non-nuclear weapons. The task, for instance, of countering an attack when the missiles are already under way would involve the formidable task of destroying, individually, thousands of re-entry vehicles. This is not practically feasible by using nuclear weapons. Other methods that are being considered by military planners include high-energy lasers and neutral particle beams. These would have to be based in space, either in low-earth or synchronous orbit, so that the beam could be directed at the multiplicity of targets during the few minutes available for their destruction. This would in any case require the destruction of many hundreds of targets within a few hundred seconds, from a range of 10,000 km. to 40,000 km.

Laser beams could beat the surface of a missile in space, while energetic particle beams may penetrate deeply into the missile and interfere with the electronics, melt fissile material, etc. However, it is an open question whether energy in amounts likely to damage a re-entry vehicle or a rocket booster could be delivered in the short time available to destroy hundreds of offensive weapons in a few minutes. This task would also require an entire system of warning, assessment, direction, command, control, energy supply, and the like. Furthermore, this sytem would have to operate under conditions when it, too, would most probably be brought under attack.

Both laser- and particle-beam systems are currently in an explorative research stage. However, strong doubts have been expressed that any of these techniques would ever be useful for an operational defence against ballistic missiles.

In the past 15 years, there has been a vast improvement in the quality and availability of anti-aircraft systems. This includes surface-to-air missile systems as well as fighter aircraft equipped with air-to-air missiles. In either case the missiles home against their targets by the use of infrared radiation or radar, some missiles carrying their own active radar and some only detectors of the radar reflections from the target caused by an illuminating beam on the ground or in the attacking aircraft.

Whether these new systems could counter aircraft delivering nuclear weapons would depend on the relative numbers of weapons and on the acceptable numbers of penetrators. Thus, it would be quite difficult to have an air defence system capable of countering the planned 3,000-ALCM United States nuclear force if it were directed against industrial targets in the Soviet Union. On the other hand, it would be a much easier task to counter manned bombers flying over and attacking fields of ICBM silos.

SLBM-launching submarines could be imperilled either by an attack while they are in port, by area search on the open ocean, or by being trailed. Submarines are highly vulnerable in port. As an example, one might consider the not uncommon occurrence of three submarines simultaneously in a particular port, with each submarine housing 16 missiles, each with 10 MIRVs. These 480 MIRVs could be destroyed by one single megaton weapon, an exchange ratio of 480 warheads for 1. But submarines on the open ocean remain quite invulnerable, despite very large annual expenditures for research and development on antisubmarine warfare techniques. This is mainly due to the difficulties inherent in their detection and localization.

As has been already stated, satellites for guidance or other purposes are likely to increase further in importance and may thus increasingly become objects for hostile action in case of a super-Power conflict. Systems for the destruction of or physical interference with satellites can be of either the direct ascent or the co-orbital type. Direct ascent systems require much less propulsion but require very great accuracy in timing and guidance, since the crossing velocity can be 10 km. per second. Co-orbital systems allow much more time. They use a multi-stage rocket put into the same orbit as the target satellite and which is manoeuvred to approach and destroy the target satellite.

One might also imagine the use of ground-based lasers, equipped with large telescope mirrors, in order to focus radiant energy on satellites in low orbit as they pass overhead. It is entirely feasible to injure sensors in satellites by ground-based lasers, although the pointing requirements are severe, the required illumination time is long (many seconds), and one must wait perhaps several days until the laser site is within a few hundred kilometres of the satellite ground track.

The Soviet Union has tested and demonstrated an anti-satellite system placed in low earth orbit. This is a non-nuclear system, in which a killer satellite would rendezvous with the target satellite and destroy it. The United States has initiated a programme to obtain an anti-satellite capability. The United States and the USSR are also continuing talks aimed towards a treaty to ban or control anti-satellite activities.

Ever since radio and electronics have been used in warfare, electronic countermeasures have been important for misleading radars, jamming radio communications and the like. Much of this capability is closely held. It is known, however, that in many cases, communication links can be rendered useless if enough jamming power is concentrated on the receiving antenna.

In the context of nuclear weapons, there is the possibility of jamming or disruption of the command and control communications to the weapons, and also of nullifying the performance of anti-aircraft or anti-satellite systems. It is possible here only to emphasize the uncertainty as to whether electronic countermeasures can deny the direct capability and whether counter-countermeasures can nullify the countermeasures.

Detection and identification systems

Such systems are useful only if the warning and assessment which they give can be acted upon to engage active or passive defences, to move weapons and other objects of attack from vulnerable postures to less vulnerable ones, to launch on warning those weapons which might otherwise be destroyed, and to determine the origin of and responsibility for an attack. It is of particular interest to note how little time in reality is available for all of this.

Land-based systems deployed in the target area have little to offer against an attack by ICBM. Forward-deployed systems, such as the ballistic missile early-warning system "BMEWS", can provide 15 minutes' warning, as can the high-performance early-warning radars in the Soviet Union. In general, the role of detection, identification and tracking of incoming missiles is divided between satellites, which can detect launching of ballistic missiles mainly through infrared sensors, and various airborne or land-based radar systems which are employed to track their trajectory.

Similarly, the "PAVE PAWS" coastal radars in the United States can give at least five minutes' warning before impact of SLBM missiles launched from the Atlantic. The so-called OTH (Over The Horizon) radar, which utilizes the reflection of electromagnetic waves against ionospheric layers, could possibly detect both ballistic missiles and low-flying aircraft or cruise missiles at very long range, although with poor accuracy. Different types of OTH radar systems are now believed to be in operation. Currently used ground-based air-defence radars can assess the threat from aircraft penetrating the airspace, and serve to alert anti-aircraft systems. Greater warning is available, however, from airborne or space-based systems.

It is well known that there exist satellite systems in high earth orbit with the primary purpose of detecting and assessing mass ICBM and SLBM raids. These satellites contain a scanning infrared detector and must construct and report trajectories of missiles in boost phase, made visible by the hundreds of kilowatts of infrared emission from the rocket engine. The observation of such raids onboard the satellite must then be transmitted to ground stations and forwarded to the national command authority. Presumably, if an adversary launches ICBMs and SLBMs, he will not refrain from an attempt to interfere with the communications from the infrared-detection satellite to the ground station. Thus, such a system must reckon with defence against jamming and against physical attack on the ground station.

It should be mentioned here that particular emphasis has been given in recent years to national technical means of verification for monitoring provisions of the United States-USSR SALT agreements. These means consist of observation satellites of various types (including photographic satellites) which have the ability to detect, identify and count missile launchers, observe submarines under construction, etc. As SALT II is intended to control various qualitative aspects of strategic forces, the "national technical means" must include ground-based and space-based sensors, which, e.g., help to determine missile mass and numbers of MIRVs.

The primary use of airborne systems is to detect and identify enemy bombers and cruise missiles. For a decade or more, it has been possible to detect aircraft by airborne radar over water, but only in the last few years has the capability existed to detect aircraft by means of airborne radar against the background land clutter. The most advanced system for performing this feat is the United States so-called AWACS aircraft, a modified commercial jet aircraft mounting a large microwave radar, and equipped as well with command and control equipment. In principle, an AWACS at 12,000 m. altitude could see even low-flying aircraft out to about 400 km., and could assign fighter aircraft, determine whether missiles launched against the penetrating aircraft had destroyed those aircraft, etc. However, many such aircraft patrolling simultaneously would be needed to detect effectively and to identify nuclear armed bombers or cruise missile carriers.

There are sea-based systems comprising acoustic detectors and arrays emplaced on the ocean bottom for monitoring the passage of submarine forces, but not much is publicly known about their performance. However, both the Soviet Union and the United States continue to build and operate SLBM submarines; they would not do so if they were not confident of the continued survival of the SLBMs during nuclear war. Intensive research continues on both sides to detect SLBM submarines, but also to ensure that there is no capability available to the other side which can imperil one's own SLBM fleet. Non-acoustic techniques continue to be studied, based on the disturbance of magnetic fields, hydrodynamic fields and the like.

Anti-submarine warfare (ASW) technology has advanced incrementally, relying primarily on passive acoustic detection of the noise emitted by submarines, with fixed hydrophones on the ocean bottom, on sonobuoys dropped by aircraft, and on sonars mounted on or towed by surface ships and submarines. The advances in electronic and information processing have facilitated this improved ASW capability, only in part compensated by submarine quietening programmes. Similarly, the application of modern science to magnetometers has allowed the detection of submarines at ranges approaching 1 km. All of this, however, is more useful in tactical anti-submarine warfare than in hunting and destroying on short notice a large, strategic SLBM fleet.

Thus far, no effective detection technique appears to have been found which would imperil the SLBM fleet. If such a technique were discovered, in most cases measures could be taken to counter it. For instance, an acoustic detection technique could be countered by the deployment of large numbers of noise sources in the ocean, either to raise the noise level or to simulate the presence of submarines. In times of war, noise echoes from nuclear explosions in the ocean basin could also be used to mark the presence of strategic submarines for a period of days.

Regional nuclear forces

IRBM and MRBM missiles forces are also being further developed. In the USSR, the SS-20 IRBMs are equipped with three MIRVs and deployed in a mobile mode. In 1979, NATO approved the principle of development and deployment of the advanced Pershing ballistic missile, as well as the ground-launched cruise missiles (GLCM). Both Pershing and GLCM are expected to obtain a lower vulnerability by means of mobile basing, giving a smaller chance of detection and a longer range.

Generally speaking, aerodynamic missiles of various sizes, ranges and basing modes could become much more prevalent in theatre nuclear forces, if that development is not checked. Many sea-launched aerodynamic missiles already exist, primarily for conventional attack on surface shipping, although they could also be used for nuclear attack on land targets. Not only the United States and the USSR but also France, Israel and other countries have such sea-based cruise missiles.

Delivery systems other than missiles are also subject to evolution, although perhaps to a less significant degree. For instance, nuclear-capable artillery is successively acquiring longer ranges, higher accuracy and greater mobility, largely as a by-product of the technological development of conventional ordnance.

There are indications that the introduction of highly efficient, precision-guided conventional missiles or other munitions ("smart weapons") might render the tactical nuclear option less attractive to military commanders in the future. Conversely, the adaptation of small nuclear warheads to precision-guided carriers could increase the effectiveness in a conflict of "surgical" nuclear strikes against field fortifications and similar targets.

In a world of nuclear-weapon proliferation, nations with small numbers of nuclear weapons would probably rely on aircraft in limited numbers and of modest performance for a delivery vehicle. There would, however, be the problem of the vulnerability of such aircraft before take-off and in their penetration of enemy airspace to reach their targets. A nuclear force largely based on aircraft with gravity bombs or unsophisticated missiles may thus not be a very stable deterrent.

IV

Effects of the Use of Nuclear Weapons

NUCLEAR WEAPONS ARE WEAPONS of mass destruction. Their various effects may cover vast areas and the destruction of the intended target within this area, whether military or civilian, can be made as complete as desired through the choice of weapon yield and the point of explosion. There is therefore no target strong enough to resist the intense effects of nuclear weapons, no effective defense against a determined attack. Protection in a nuclear war, when it exists, does so because of limits imposed on the strength of the attack. In this sense, mankind is faced with the absolute weapon.

At the same time, it is the very strength of the effects of nuclear explosives that make them difficult to use as war-fighting weapons in the traditional sense. It is a fact that there are today megaton weapons in existence each of which releases an energy greater than that of all conventional explosives ever used since gunpowder was invented. If this enormous power were ever to be used, the consequences in terms of human casualties and physical destruction would be virtually incomprehensible. Figures and rough estimates may be given, as indeed they will in the following, but there exists an uncertain limit beyond which such data have little meaning except as a categorical imperative that nuclear war must never happen.

The existing knowledge of the effects of the use of nuclear

weapons is far from complete. Although numerous tests have been carried out, forming a basis for the understanding of the physical explosion phenomena, there are only two instances when these weapons have been used in war, on 6 August 1945 against Hiroshima and on 9 August 1945 against Nagasaki. The outcome of these explosions has been painstakingly investigated, in particular with regard to the number of people killed or injured, and yet considerably different data are given by different sources, as will be illustrated below.

Furthermore, any assessment of a hypothetical future situation based on the Japanese data would have to rest on interpretation and sometimes extrapolation, as today's arsenals contain weapons that are a thousand times more powerful than the two used in Japan, but also smaller and, in some cases, specialized weapons (cf. chapter II). Thus there are uncertainties as to the effects of one single explosion.

It is a well-established fact that the explosion of a nuclear weapon causes damage through several effects: a powerful blast wave, intense heat radiation and nuclear radiation from the fireball and from radioactive fallout. There is also a pulse of electromagnetic radiation not directly harmful to living creatures. However, the size of the area affected by these various phenomena, their strength—in absolute terms and relative to each other—and the extent of the damage they cause will depend strongly on the explosive yield but also on a number of other factors specific to each situation. Among these are the height above ground of the explosion, weather conditions and (particulary for explosions close to the ground) wind velocity and, of course, the nature of target. The design of the weapon will also influence the outcome.

Should large numbers of nuclear weapons ever come to be used, the total effect would be much more complex than the sum of individual cases. This is in some part due to interactions of a direct and physical nature, for instance on electrical or other networks, but the most important additional uncertainties pertain to the over-all social, economic and political consequences of the sudden and widespread devastation that a nuclear war would

entail. The accounts given below should therefore be considered
only as probable indications of the magnitude of the effects of
nuclear war.

These accounts start with a brief overview of the physical
effects of a nuclear explosion, which are more fully treated in
appendix I. To render the description less abstract, some numerical values are given which relate to a weapon yield similar to those
of the bombs against Japan. A few subsequent examples aim at
illustrating the effects of larger yield weapons against cities.

The next three sections describe the destructive power of
nuclear weapons when applied to different war scenarios. The
first section deals with a limited nuclear attack, addressing some
rather theoretical cases of nuclear violence between nuclear-
weapon States and then exploring the possible results of nuclear
aggression against a non-nuclear-weapon State. The next section
attempts—in one simplified example—an analysis of the consequences if theatre nuclear weapons were to be extensively used in
a super-Power conflict. The last major section, which draws on
the voluminous United States literature on the subject, is a con-
densed treatment of the counterforce and counter-value types of
strategic nuclear exchange between the super-Powers but also
indicates some of the global consequences, including the social
and economic ones, that might follow from a large-scale nuclear
war. In some of these contexts, reference is made to different protective measures, in particular civil defence, which is dealt with in
more detail at the end of the chapter.

Effects of one nuclear explosion
A weapon of moderate yield

When a nuclear weapon is exploded above ground, the first
noticeable effect is a blinding flash of intense white light, strong
enough to temporarily blind or at least dazzle observers out to
many kilometres distant from the explosion. The general impression is that the whole sky is brilliantly illuminated. The light is
emitted from the surface of the "fireball", a roughly spherical
mass of very hot air (the temperature is of the order of 10 million

degrees centigrade) and weapon residues, which develops quickly around the exploding weapon and continues to grow until it reaches a maximum radius which depends on the yield. For a weapon with a yield of 10 to 20 kt., i.e., that of the Hiroshima and Nagasaki bombs, the maximum radius is approximately 200 m. and its development takes about one second. During that time, and for some time after, the fireball emits thermal radiation both as light and—mainly—heat. Finally, the thermal radiation dies away as the fireball is cooled and transformed into the mushroom-shaped explosion cloud. By then, about one third of the explosive energy has been released as heat.

Within and close to the fireball, everything will evaporate or melt. At some distance from the explosion the two most important effects of thermal radiation will be to cause burns ("flash burns") on exposed skin and to ignite fires. Second-degree burns to unprotected skin may occur 3 km. from the explosion, and at 2 km. third-degree burns will be frequent. (Second-degree burns cause pain and blisters. Third-degree burns, where parts of the skin are destroyed, cause disfiguring scars called cheloids.) At less than 2 km., thermal radiation can be expected to kill most people directly exposed to it. Materials that are easily ignited, such as thin fabrics, paper or dry leaves, may catch fire at more than 2 km. from ground-zero. This may cause numerous fires, which under some conditions may form a huge fire storm enveloping much of the target area and adding numerous further casualties. That was the case in Hiroshima, although it is considered less likely in modern cities.

Often the most important effect of a nuclear explosion is the blast wave, which is similar to that of a chemical explosion but differs quantitatively owing to the much larger amount of energy involved. The air blast carries about half the explosive energy (cf. Fig. VI) and travels much slower than the various forms of radiation, but—for the yield chosen here—in about one and a half seconds it reaches a 1 km. circle around ground-zero and in 5 or 6 seconds it has expanded to 3 km. The arrival of the blast wave is experienced as a sudden and shattering blow, immediately fol-

Nuclear Weapons and War

Figure VI. Distribution of Energy in an Air Burst of a Fission Weapon at an Altitude of Less Than 30,000 m. (100,000 feet)

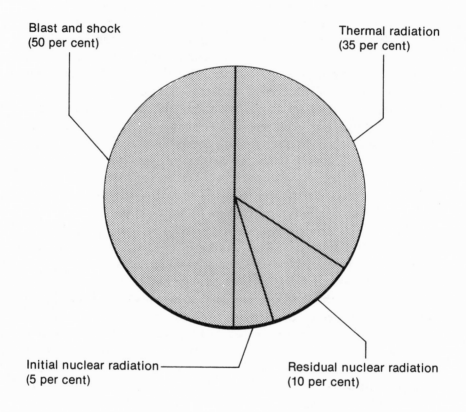

Blast and shock
(50 per cent)

Thermal radiation
(35 per cent)

Initial nuclear radiation
(5 per cent)

Residual nuclear radiation
(10 per cent)

lowed by a hurricane-force wind directed outwards from the explosion. Out to perhaps 1.5 km. from ground-zero, where the maximum wind speed will be about 90 m./sec. (three times "full gale" by the meteorological definition), the blast wind may uproot trees, blow down telephone and utility poles and overturn even heavy (civilian) vehicles. Virtually all buildings will be utterly demolished. Persons standing in the open will be swept up by the wind and carried with it along the surface of the ground, hitting other objects and being hit by loose, flying debris which acts as projectiles, killing or injuring people. Out to a distance of at least 2 km. most buildings will be crushed by the compressional load as they are engulfed by the blast overpressure and the wind drag. People inside may be crushed under the weight of the falling buildings, hurt by the flying debris of broken windows, furniture, etc., or even suffocated by the dense dust of crushed brick and mortar. Especially in houses that are partially damaged, fires may start from overturned stoves and fires, broken gas lines, etc., causing further casualties among the population. A very rough estimate is that within the 1.5 km. circle, the blast will kill—by various mechanisms—virtually everybody in the open or in ordinary buildings. All the primary blast destruction has taken place during a few seconds.

Even before any visible phenomena occur, the exploding device starts to emit an intense burst of neutrons and gamma rays. This radiation is attenuated with distance as it is propagated through the air, but at 700 or 800 m. from ground-zero of a 15 kt. burst it is still strong enough to render human beings in the open unconscious within minutes. In practice most of them would be killed by blast or heat, but even if these effects did not exist they would die in less than one or two days from the radiation injury. The radiation received at a distance of 1,300-1,400 m. will also be fatal but death may be delayed up to about a month. At larger distances the radiation hazard decreases rapidly, and at about 1,800 m. or more from ground-zero few if any acute radiation injuries are expected to occur. Virtually all of this radiation is released during the first one or two seconds.

Simultaneously, a small part of the gamma ray energy is converted to electromagnetic energy through interaction with the surrounding air. A strong electromagnetic field develops around the explosion and disappears again in less than a millisecond. During its brief existence this field radiates electromagnetic waves in approximately the same manner as a radio transmitter aerial, and any kind of electrical conductor may act as an antenna and pick up some of the electromagnetic energy. In this manner currents may be induced which can damage many types of electric and—in particular—electronic equipment.

Some of the neutrons emitted from the explosion will give rise to nuclear reactions by which radioactive atoms are created in the weapon residues and the air but also in the soil around ground-zero and in some other materials that may be hit by the radiation. This induced radioactivity is in general negligible compared to fallout activity.

When the fireball rises, it cools off and is gradually transformed into a huge cloud. A column of dust and smoke sucked up from the ground forms the stem of the "mushroom". After some 10 minutes when the cloud is fully developed, it will have a diameter of 4-6 km., while the base is perhaps 6 and the top 10 km. above the ground.

The fireball, and later the cloud, contains most of the radioactive atoms, mostly fission products, that were formed in the explosion. While the total weight of these fragments is small, about 1 kg., their combined radioactivity one hour after the explosion equals that of several thousand tons of radium (although the emitted radiation is somewhat different). This activity decays rapidly, however; during the first two weeks it decreases to one thousandth of what it was one hour after the explosion. Included in the cloud is also much of the original fissile material used in the nuclear weapon, notably uranium-235 or plutonium-239, and activities induced in weapon materials or in surrounding matter, including the air. These may constitute more long-lasting hazards as the half-lives of some of these nuclides range from tens of thousands to hundreds of millions of years. As the cloud develops, the radioactive atoms are incorporated in larger particles formed by condensing vapours and mixed-in dust and dirt. The range of the radiation is relatively short compared to either the height of the cloud base or the size of the devastated area. For this reason, the radioactive particles in the cloud do not constitute a health hazard until they are deposited on the ground as radioactive fallout.

The radioactive cloud drifts, changes shape and eventually disintegrates under the action of the winds at those altitudes where it stabilized. At the same time, the particles carrying the activity subside with speeds which depend strongly on their size. In the case of an air burst, most particles will be very small and it may take from days to years for them to reach the ground. By that time they have lost most of their radioactivity and have been scattered over a wide area. Fallout over intermediate times may be denoted tropospheric, while the very slow deposition of particles injected into the stratosphere is usually referred to as global fallout. This fallout radiation does not cause any acute ill effects, but over the decades to follow, some tens of cases (for a 10-20 kt. yield) of "late effects" (additional cancers and genetic injuries) may occur. In other instances, as in Nagasaki, some radioactivity may be deposited on the ground of the target area by rainfall induced by or coincident with the explosion. An increase in the acute and late effects is then to be expected.

When the nuclear weapon explodes at or close to the ground, with the fireball in direct contact with the surface, thousands of tons of soil are injected into the hot vapours. Large (diameters up to one millimetre or more) particles then carry a significant part of the residual radioactivity. These particles come down to earth in a matter of hours or even minutes and create an intensely radioactive contamination field in the downwind vicinity of ground-zero. After a 10 to 20 kt. ground burst this so-called immediate fallout gives rise to acutely lethal radiation doses for unprotected people over an area of 50-100 km². As a result, the possibility of late radiation injuries in this area is also much larger than in the case of an air burst.

The specific nuclear-weapon characteristics in the over-all range of effects against human beings, aside from the high incidence of thermal burns, are these acute and late radiation injuries. At high dose levels, the radiation will render the victim unconscious after a few minutes and cause death within a couple of days, during which the victim may or may not have regained consciousness. For lower but still lethal doses, the onset of ill effects will be slower and less dramatic, and death may not come until after several weeks. Acute radiation sickness caused by non-lethal doses could trail off with a state of general weakness protracted over months and years.

Those surviving an acute radiation injury will stand a larger risk than do others of disease with certain forms of cancer. This risk is considered proportional to the dose received. The disease could remain latent for decades before becoming manifest. Even if the radiation exposure was not large enough to cause a state of acute sickness, there might follow an increased risk of late cancer. The same is believed to hold true for genetic or hereditary effects brought about by irradiation of the reproductive organs. In both these instances, however, there are differences of opinion among scientists as to the numerical estimates of the risk.

The total number of casualties and the extent of material damage that are the result of one nuclear explosion may vary widely depending on a number of factors, some of which are not fully understood. According to one source[13] the Hiroshima bomb, estimated to be 13 kt., caused the death of about 70,000 civilians within a month, and some further 80,000 were injured. A larger bomb, 22 kt., against Nagasaki gave casualties of 40,000 and 20,000 correspondingly. The discrepancy between the two outcomes has been ascribed to the different topographies of the two cities. In Nagasaki there are a number of ridges separating different parts of the city, which lead to a lower average population density and to some weakening of the air in certain areas. Within the 1 km. radius from ground-zero, however, the casualties (dead and injured) were about 95 per cent of the total population in both cases, with a somewhat higher incidence of fatalities in Nagasaki.

In a report which the mayors of Hiroshima and Nagasaki prepared in 1976, the following figures are mentioned. In the case of Hiroshima, between 310,000 and 320,000 people were exposed to the various effects of the atomic explosion. Of these, between 130,000 and 150,000 had died by December 1945 and an estimated 200,000 by 1950, if latent effects are included. In Nagasaki, the corresponding numbers are 270,000-280,000, 60,000-80,000 and 100,000. The lack of exact numbers is due to uncertainties about the number of military and other personnel in the cities on the days of attack, as well as the destruction and unavailability of relevant records because of the attack. Cases of genetic effects, and latent exposure on those who entered the two cities after the days of attack, are also reported. The death toll was still increasing, although very slowly, even in 1979, although it is not easy to relate cause and effect so many years after the actual atomic bomb explosions.

If the same size of weapon were used against a large city like New York and the weapon exploded without any warning, a very crude estimate based on scaling the Hiroshima figures would give between 500,000 and 1 million immediate casualties, of which 200,000 might be killed at once (see Fig. VII). The actual figures would depend on a number of unknowns, among which the most important probably are the time of day and day of the week. During office hours, for instance, casualties could be well above the level of 1 million.

High-kiloton and megaton explosions over cities

All the figures given above for distances, sizes, times and so forth will increase or decrease with the explosive yield but in less than direct proportion to the yield. Roughly speaking, tenfold or hundredfold increases in yield give, respectively, fivefold and twentyfold increases of the area devastated by air blast. Conversely one might say that the "overkill" close to ground-zero is larger, the larger the yield. This does not mean, however, that single high-yield explosions do not cause horrendous devastation.

Figure VII. A Hiroshima Bomb Over New York

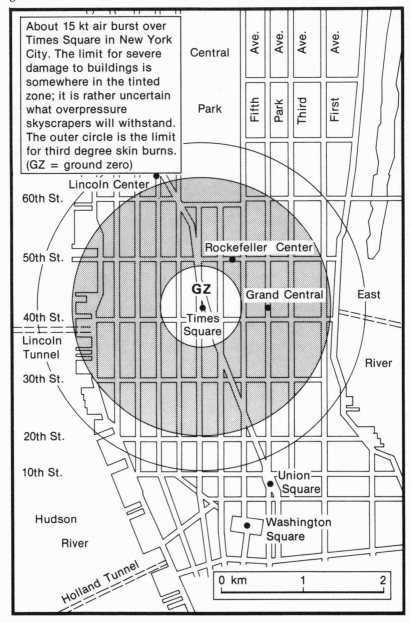

About 15 kt air burst over Times Square in New York City. The limit for severe damage to buildings is somewhere in the tinted zone; it is rather uncertain what overpressure skyscrapers will withstand. The outer circle is the limit for third degree skin burns. (GZ = ground zero)

If, for instance, a 100 kt. low airburst occurred over the centre of a European city with half a million inhabitants, this could kill up to half the population by immediate effects, if no warning had been given. The zone where at least 50 per cent of all buildings would be destroyed by blast would have a radius of 5 to 6 km. As for the effect on small one-family houses, which are more frequent on the outskirts of the city, the radius might be even greater. Over approximately the same distance, the thermal radiation would ignite fires, some of which would grow and spread, causing further material destruction as well as additional deaths. Within less than an hour after the explosion, large parts of the 2-to-6 km. zone might be ablaze, while parts of the area inside 2 km. might be sites for slow, creeping fire in the heaps of rubble created by the air blast. In comparison to blast and thermal effects, initial neutron and gamma radiation would be less significant, because the dangerous area for initial nuclear radiation is inside the circle where, as a rule, people would be killed by blast or heat. Radiation might, however, add somewhat to the casualty figures, and also diminish prospects for recovery among survivors with mechanical injuries or burns.

The number of fatalities and level of destruction in a city under nuclear attack depend on many factors, of which those related to civil defence preparedness are discussed later in this chapter. Other important parameters are the size of the city and the distribution of its population in relation to weapon yield, the height of burst and ground-zero location (see also Fig. IX).

In addition to the immediate effects, survivors face many additional difficulties. Water and electricity services would operate far below standards or fail altogether, heating would have broken down, food supplies would be scarce and medical care facilities hopelessly inadequate. Telecommunications with the outside would be seriously disrupted because of blast and thermal effects and electromagnetic pulse. Key industrial installations in the city would be rendered largely inoperative in a nuclear attack.

If the weapon had exploded as a ground burst, more than 100 square kilometres would be contaminated by radioactive fallout strong enough to give people fatal doses within a week, unless special precautions were taken. This heavily contaminated area would extend downwind from the explosion to far outside the city proper, covering less densely populated districts but also with less radiation shielding. The over-all short-term losses due to fallout radiation could be in the range of 5,000 to 20,000 people for a typical European country. As in the previous example, a number of late radiation deaths would have to be added.

For a country in another part of the world—in particular a developing tropical country—the consequences might be even worse. In cities like Bombay, Cairo or Hong Kong a 100 kt. low air burst might immediately kill well over a million people, as compared to about 200,000 in the example above. The primary reason for this would be the high population density in these cities. Possibly, the average robustness of buildings would also be lower than in European cities, leading to blast devastation in a larger zone.

As was indicated in chapter II, many strategic warheads in the two super-Powers have a yield of one megaton or more. These weapons are powerful enough to wreak almost complete destruction on any city, save for a few of the world's largest urban conglomerates.

For these very large weapons, the thermal effects are even more predominant in the total picture (although blast is still the major cause of material destruction). The fireball from a 1 Mt. explosion in air continues to grow for more than 10 seconds. Eventually it reaches a radius of almost 1 km., and by that time it has emitted, as thermal radiation, more energy than a 1,000 MW power plant produces in two weeks, scorched an area in excess of 250 km² and blinded (permanently or temporarily) people out to perhaps 50 km. from the explosion (much farther at night). The mushroom cloud that is subsequently formed reaches a height of about 20 km. and approximately the same diameter.

A recent study[14] by the Office of Technical Assessment (OTA) of the United States Congress described the effects of a 1 Mt. explosion over the centre of a city with about 4 million inhabitants (Detroit or Leningrad). Some of the conclusions were:

(a) That an air burst (height 1,800 m.) at night would immediately kill about half a million people and injure an additional 600,000 in Detroit;

(b) That the corresponding figures for Leningrad are about double those for Detroit, the reason being the (estimated) demographic differences between the two cities;

(c) That the area in which houses would be completely demolished, blown out or otherwise rendered uninhabitable would exceed 300 km²;

(d) That the incidence of burn injuries (many of them eventually fatal) among survivors of the blast could vary from some thousands up to several hundreds of thousands, depending on the number of people exposed to the line of sight from the fireball and on atmospheric visibility.

With this large yield, the initial nuclear radiation will cause very few additional fatalities or injuries. On the other hand, radioactive fallout with a radiation intensity sufficient to be acutely harmful would contaminate an area probably in excess of 1,000 km², if the explosion were a surface burst. In a much larger area there would occur delayed radiation injuries. It should be noted in passing that the OTA study also found that the combined effects of 10 40-kt. weapons, with ground-zeros about 2 km. apart, exceeded those of the single 1 Mt. weapon, in particular with regard to the number of people immediately killed.

Considering finally an explosion of 10 to 20 Mt. with the same ground-zero in New York as the 10 to 20 kt. explosion discussed above, this would destroy all buildings not only in Manhattan, but also in almost all of the Bronx, Brooklyn and Queens, as far as Kennedy Airport, and in Hoboken and Jersey City as well (see Fig. VIII). Even more devastating than the air blast, however, would be the thermal radiation. Second-degree burns could be expected to occur out to about 40 km. from ground-zero; the corresponding area would be almost twice that of serious blast

Figure VIII. 15 Mt Air Burst Over New York

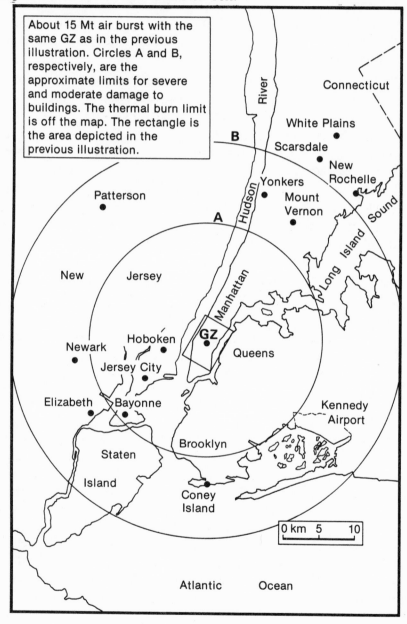

damage. The number of casualties is difficult to estimate. It would certainly be in excess of 5 million but not over 10 million.

For an explosion at ground surface with this yield, there happens to be an experimental observation regarding the extent of the fallout area. According to official United States sources,[15] the 15 Mt. test explosion code-named CASTLE BRAVO and carried out at Bikini Atoll on 1 March 1954 "caused substantial contamination over an area of more than 7,000 square miles". (This area, roughly 18,000 km², would not correspond exactly to those indicated above, however, as "substantial contamination" is believed to be, in this tropical and peacetime context, anything that would cause a non-zero risk of acute radiation injury during weeks of exposure in open air.)

To sum up the effects of a nuclear weapon explosion on a city and focusing on cities in the 0.1-1 million inhabitants range (to which indeed most cities in the world belong), the diagram in Fig. IX was constructed. It has been drawn assuming a surprise attack with one weapon, exploded at a height chosen to optimize the area of blast destruction to ordinary residential houses and with ground-zero in the geometrical centre of the city, and further assuming that the population is evenly distributed over the city's area. The diagram shows, for three population densities, the weapon yields which cause roughly 50 per cent fatalities in medium-sized cities.

Effects of a limited nuclear attack[16]

The term "limited nuclear attack" can be interpreted only in a specific context. In general, however, the term implies a certain degree of restraint in the execution of an attack, thus limiting the damage. It is open to debate whether a nuclear war between the major nuclear Powers could be conducted with such restraint, and there will always be a very large risk of escalation. However, some studies refer to "limited attacks" in a central strategic context, and this subject will be reviewed in a later section.

In addition, one could conceive of other "limited" scenarios, which might have less likelihood but which are technically feasi-

Figure IX. Destructive Capability of Nuclear Weapons When Employed Against Cities

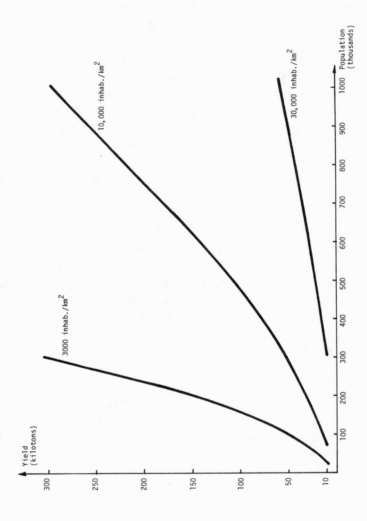

Weapon yields that could kill immediately half the population in a medium-sized city, as a function of city size and population density. (Cf. also main text)

ble and occasionally mentioned in the literature. These will be the topic of this section. Some of them are clearly related to a super-Power conflict, but the majority pertain to nuclear aggression against non-nuclear-weapon States. If nuclear weapons are further proliferated, and if no interventions or other sanctions have to be feared, that sort of aggression might become a realistic alternative in future conflicts. In those hypothetical cases, nuclear weapons use may be limited because the aggressor has limited nuclear means.

At present, however, the basic situation would be one where a State with an abundance of nuclear weapons decided to use some of these weapons to enforce its will upon a non-nuclear-weapon State. (To decide to do so, one would require a virtual certainty that the action did not trigger a large nuclear conflict.) In this case, other limitations could apply.

Such limitations should not be thought of as simply a matter of the number of weapons employed, as the launching of even one nuclear weapon represents a most serious decision. Political and military constraints would most probably apply to the decision and determine what restrictions might exist concerning the nature and location of the targets. This could, for instance, imply that certain areas or certain types of facility would be excluded from targeting. There could thus be large differences in the consequences of various hypothetical nuclear attacks, but there is no distinct gap between the different categories. The consequences for the victim may vary from the slightest to the most severe.

The lowest level of nuclear violence could be an implicit or outspoken threat to use nuclear weapons. Such a threat could next be emphasized by means of a "demonstration explosion" giving only some slight effects on the ground and delayed radiation effects from global fallout. Or a target could be chosen, so located that a nuclear weapon could destroy it without causing any appreciable immediate damage to other areas. Such "solitary" targets could be satellites in space, ships at sea, remote air or naval bases and isolated military or commercial installations.

Satellite nuclear warfare, which would be mainly an affair

between the super-Powers, would involve high-altitude bursts, creating electromagnetic pulse damage over large parts of the earth's surface (and hence possibly for many uninvolved nations), and late effects from global fallout. Long-range radio communications might be disturbed for an extended period of time, and power or telephone shutdowns could occur locally or regionally. Many of the other types of target indicated above would be destroyed by fairly low yield weapons. In particular, surface vessels at sea are relatively "easy" targets for modern guided missiles and could be sunk immediately with a small nuclear warhead.

There is in modern military literature some discussion regarding procedures and planning for the use of nuclear weapons against military targets in a zone of combat and possibly military and military support targets over a larger area (a "theatre of war"). The planning is done within a framework of tactical and military policy considerations regarding guidelines for the use of nuclear and conventional resources in a theatre of war. But this would in turn be subject to decisions at a political level as to whether nuclear weapons should be used at all and if so, in what manner.

In general, the employment of nuclear weapons against military targets would produce considerable "collateral" (i.e., unintended and undesired) damage to large areas of civilian society, particularly if surface bursts were used. This would occur even if political directives emphasized the importance of avoiding collateral damage as far as possible.

As an example of "limited-theatre use" of nuclear weapons, one might assume that military operations were launched in the face of defending ground forces with a strength of four army divisions (around 80,000 men). The ground defence might be supported by approximately 100 aircraft operating from 10 or more bases. This is a significant defence, yet one possessed by many non-nuclear-weapon States. To break through by conventional force only, a traditional estimate is that an attacker must assign at least 12 army divisions[17] and several hundred aircraft to the operation. The same result could be achieved by using some tens of weapons of 1 to 10 kt. yield against important elements of the ground forces and up to 10 weapons of 20 to 100 kt. yield to reduce the opponent's air force.

For each of the low-yield shots against army units in the field immediate civilian casualties would vary within wide limits, with a possible average of about 1,000 (in a fairly densely populated rural district). A total of 50,000 to 100,000 dead or severely injured civilians due to the direct effects could be the outcome of this part of the campaign. The attacks on air force bases would perhaps add another 100,000 people to these figures, especially if some of these bases were also ordinary airports, relatively close to population centres.

In addition, it is likely some of the strikes would be (intentionally or otherwise) surface bursts causing severe radioactive contamination in some areas. Under assumptions believed to be realistic, regarding the radiation-shielding properties of ordinary buildings and time spent outdoors, this could mean anything between 10,000 and 50,000 additional radiation casualties.[18]

Assuming some intermediate values in the ranges indicated, the total sum of fatalities and severe injuries in this campaign could come out as follows:

Cause	Civilian	Military
Immediate nuclear-weapon effects	150,000	30,000
Fallout radiation	30,000	5,000
Total	180,000	35,000

If some protective measures were considered, in terms of possible evacuation, warning and access to shelters, the casualties could be reduced by a factor of 3-5. There is a very wide margin of error to these figures. However, this does not invalidate the most conspicuous conclusion that can be drawn from the table: even when only military targets are selected, and even if protection is provided, the civilian casualties may far outnumber the military ones.

Other immediate effects, which could add to the number of

casualties and create additional difficulties during a rescue period, would include disruption of medical care, of power and telecommunication networks and of ground and air transport; tree felling and possibly forest fires; and, to a lesser extent, induced radioactivity in the ground near the explosion points. In addition to the immediate consequences, there would be several thousands of late radiation deaths over several decades, and a similar number of genetic effects. (Some of these would occur outside the attacked country.) Agricultural and industrial activity could certainly be seriously disrupted, but to what extent and with what consequences would depend on the specific attack conditions.

In spite of the large numbers of civilians killed and injured, and in spite of other late effects (not only on health, nutrition and medical care but also on the economy and the morale of the victimized population), military planners might consider this to be a limited attack, which could be followed by another and yet another if military resistance were to continue.

If a military campaign with nuclear weapons were ever to take place in a developing country, there would be important differences with regard to the general conditions of living and their influence on collateral damage and on the potential for survival. The means available to the civilian population for their physical protection against weapons effects would be much less adequate than in a developed country. Primitive and perhaps fragile houses would afford little protection against even weak blast waves and moderate fallout. In a warm climate, scant clothing could give rise to a higher incidence of both thermal burns and skin injuries from radioactive particles in the fallout. Tree felling and large forest fires could occur in any country but would be more difficult to deal with where there was a scarcity of various kinds of equipment.

In the military discussion of nuclear war it is common practice to distinguish "strategic" nuclear weapons from "tactical" or "theatre" ones. Whereas it is true that weapons denoted "strategic" have, on the average, higher explosive yields and longer ranges than the others, it is also important to realize that the distinction does not primarily rest with the weapons themselves but with the objectives for their use.

Strategic attack is often defined as aiming at the elimination of the attacked nation as a war-fighting unit, either as a consequence of the devastation wrought upon it or because it surrenders in order to avoid further destruction. Nuclear weapons have added new dimensions to this concept. In the Second World War strategic bombing was an instrument for the attrition of the enemy's industrial potential, particularly the arms industry, and for the demoralization of the enemy population. This was a lengthy process and seen as a supplement rather than an alternative to ordinary military operations. With long-range nuclear weapons it has become possible to wreak near-complete eradication of a nation's population and devastation of its economy in less than a day's time and on less than an hour's notice. It is worth noting that even what is termed a limited nuclear attack would have the most deleterious consequences.

Another new factor is that some of the nuclear means for strategic use are themselves regarded as strategic targets. Accordingly, two different strategic modes for nuclear-weapon employment have emerged: "counterforce" against these weapons, and "counter-value" corresponding to the classical strategic attack. Possibilities and probabilities concerning the nuclear exchange between the super-Powers in either or both of these modes are extensively studied and publicly discussed. This discussion, however, should not be allowed to obscure the fact that States other than the super-Powers, including non-nuclear countries, could be targets for a nuclear strategic attack against value targets and, in effect, one using weapons other than those commonly called strategic. In the context of the power-bloc balance this is reflected by the distinction that is sometimes made between "central strategic" and "Eurostrategic" systems (cf. chapter II). But the core of the matter is that a wide spectrum of nuclear weapons can now be put to strategic use.

The effects of one nuclear explosion against a city have been described above. A limited strategic attack could, however, involve the targeting of several cities. The most important fact is then that a simple addition of casualties or destroyed facilities would not give a true picture of the extent of the devastation. After a single city attack, a national effort could conceivably be organized to rescue and aid survivors and to compensate for the loss of industrial capacity. With five major cities obliterated simultaneously and casualties in one day running to perhaps 10 per cent of the nation's population, both the physical capacity and the psychological strength to launch such an effort might be in doubt. The number of people in need of medical care would be much larger than could be coped with, not only in the targeted cities but in the entire country. Some key industrial branches might have been destroyed and this could become an immediate difficulty if, for instance, some basic foods or medical supplies were among the items that could not be produced. Administrative problems of an unprecedented nature and magnitude would arise and cause extreme difficulties for the national, regional and local governments.

Effects of extensive use of tactical nuclear weapons

At present, the most obvious danger of an extensive use of tactical or theatre nuclear weapons would exist if there were a super-Power conflict in Europe. Here there are large, diversified and militarily integrated nuclear arsenals that could be used for extensive theatre employment. In Europe, there is also the strong political commitment, the geographic proximity between bloc territories and the concentration of forces—conventional as well as nuclear—that could constitute the possible setting for a large-scale confrontation. In the future, however, similar dangers may present themselves also in other areas of the world, since the number of available weapons in the super-Power arsenal continues to increase.

If such a war should occur, the probability is that it could not be kept at theatre level. On the contrary, a crisis which had escalated beyond the use of a few theatre nuclear weapons could be in imminent danger of reaching the level of "strategic exchange", owing to the magnitude of political objectives which by necessity would underline a conflict of such tension. In particular, this could be the case if an extensive theatre nuclear war should turn out to be of considerable disadvantage to one of the two sides. A technical factor indicating the ease with which escalation could occur from the theatre to the strategic level is that the same weapon systems could be used for either purpose.

No analysis of a large-scale theatre nuclear war has so far been made public. A comprehensive study of the consequences of a nuclear war in the Federal Republic of Germany was published in 1971.[19] But it is not possible to describe the effects of a nuclear war in a detailed and accurate manner. The consequences are too vast and complex.

The situation being considered is one in which both sides had mobilized and deployed forces in the range of 50 to 100 divisions each, and where these and their supporting tactical air forces had been issued their nuclear munitions.

The assumption is further that the priority targets would be the adversary's nuclear delivery means in the theatre, i.e., field artillery, rocket and guided missile units and air bases. Thus, the exchange would basically be a duel between the opposing nuclear systems. In addition, armoured units and command posts would be targeted and rear-area targets other than army forces and air bases would not be excluded *per se*. They would be less important to the outcome of a nuclear campaign of short duration, but might still add appreciably to the number of casualties. Attacks on targets at sea might take place but would cause little collateral damage except for global fallout.

The weaponry available to the two sides is today somewhat asymmetrical. To reflect this, the average yield of weapons for battlefield targets might be 1 kt. on one side and 5 kt. on the other. It is further assumed that command and communication centres, air bases and other rear-area targets would be attacked only with missiles equipped with 100 kt. warheads. The situation described might lead to a nuclear-weapon employment as follows:

Side	Ground forces targets	Air bases, etc.
A	1,000 weapons, average yield 1 kt.	100 weapons, average yield 100 kt.
B	500 weapons, average yield 5 kt.	100 weapons, average yield 100 kt.

The ensuing civilian casualties would vary with the distribution of people in the targeted areas and the locations of ground-zeros with respect to this distribution. A lower estimate could be based on the same assumption as in the preceding section, that there were no military targets except air bases in the vicinity of major cities. For the battle area, the average population density could be 100 persons/km^2.

The worst case would occur when the shots from both sides were distributed without any regard to the civilian settlements in the battle area, i.e., non-restrictive employment. The consequences would be less severe if one or both of the belligerents were restrictive, i.e., deliberately tried to avoid hitting these settlements.

The resulting casualty figures (dead and severely injured civilians) for the employment of the low-yield weapons against ground forces can be calculated as follows:

Employment characteristics	Civilian casualties
A and B restrictive	0.1 million
A non-restrictive, B restrictive	0.5 million
A restrictive, B non-restrictive	0.6 million
A and B non-restrictive	1.0 million

The casualties would be caused by blast effects, thermal radiation and fire, initial radiation and combinations of these. One could expect that virtually all of those with severe injuries would die, as adequate medical treatment would not be available.

The major part of the collateral damage against the civilian society would not be caused by the 100 kt. weapons. Even though the targets for these weapons would not as a rule be located within urban areas and, in addition, would presumably be surrounded by an uninhabited safety zone, a population density of 300 persons/km^2 is assumed, bearing in mind that the population density in large European cities is about 10 times that figure. With this assumption, each of the 100 kt. weapons might kill or injure about 25,000 civilians, which would lead to a total of up to 5 million casualties. Thus the conclusion would be that the immediate effects of this nuclear war would be between 5 and 6 million civilian lives. This would hold only as long as the weapons were properly aimed, however. Each missile going astray and hitting an urban area instead of the intended target would add another quarter of a million to the total.

It is assumed that some of the 1,700 explosions would be surface bursts, producing local radioactive fallout, acutely hazardous to the population in areas downwind from the burst. The size of such areas, and, consequently, the number of people exposed to the hazard, would increase with the explosive yield (see Fig. X). For this reason, fallout from one of the 1 kt. or 5 kt. weapons on the battlefield would add very little to the over-all casualty figures. If no more than 10 per cent of these explosions were surface bursts, an estimate would be that 20,000 to 50,000 additional deaths would be caused by fallout therefrom. The number is highly dependent on population density and availability of shelters.

Fallout from the 200 weapons of 100 kt. would constitute a more serious problem, as each weapon would release a much larger amount of radioactivity. A larger proportion of the explosions might also be surface bursts, and the population density in the fallout areas would be higher. If half of these explosions were surface bursts, a total of about 0.7 million people could be expected to receive radiation doses causing death within about a month, even if it were assumed that they made reasonable efforts to stay in shelter.

In addition to high dose effects, there would be a number of late somatic and genetic injuries caused primarily by the fallout

Figure X. Fallout Areas From Tactical Nuclear Weapons

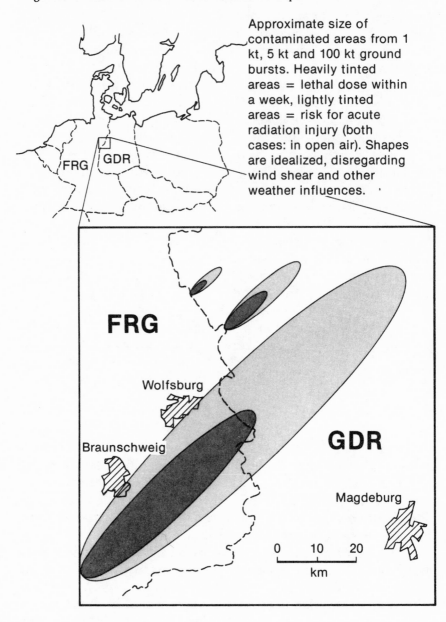

Approximate size of contaminated areas from 1 kt, 5 kt and 100 kt ground bursts. Heavily tinted areas = lethal dose within a week, lightly tinted areas = risk for acute radiation injury (both cases: in open air). Shapes are idealized, disregarding wind shear and other weather influences.

from surface bursts. These would occur over a period of some decades after the war. The number of late cancers, including leukaemia, could be about 400,000 in the countries where the explosions took place. These would mainly be caused by the 100 kt. explosions, with perhaps some 10,000 cases originating from the fallout from the lower-yield weapons or from initial radiation among those who survived the direct effects of an explosion. The total casualties are summarized in table 2.

Table 2. Total casualties (dead and severely injured) in the theatre nuclear war described in the text

Weapons (all fission):	200 x 100 kt.	1,500 x low yield	
Population density, km^{-2}:	300	100	
Percentage of surface bursts:	50	10	
Civilian			*Approx. total*
Immediate effects	5 mill.	0.1-1 mill.	5-6 million
Early fallout	0.7 mill.	0.02-0.05 mill.	0.7 million
Late radiation	0.4 mill.	0.01 mill.	0.4 million
Total civilian	6.1 mill.	0.1-1.1 mill	6-7 million
Military			
All causes			0.4 million

In the above scenario the total yield delivered (23.5 Mt.) is a small fraction of the destructive power available to the super-Powers, the individual weapon yields are all far below those which are common in the weapons denoted strategic, and targeting restrictions have been observed. Although the plausibility of the scenario may be doubted, it offers a very conservative setting for a description of possible effects of nuclear war-fighting. Nevertheless, the important point emerges that civilian casualties could hardly be reduced below a certain, very high level, given the collateral effects of the nuclear attacks against the enemy's air force and other long-range systems. In addition to the civilian casualties, large military forces would have been virtually obliterated and thousands of nuclear weapons spent (but the over-all nuclear strength of the super-Powers would still remain essentially intact). The civilian casualties would, however, outnumber the military ones by more than 12 to 1.

Effects of a total nuclear war, a nuclear exchange

A total nuclear war is the highest level of human madness. Perhaps it is, therefore, not surprising that many studies of this have been carried out, analysing the consequences in some detail. The results of course vary with the assumptions made regarding targets, the numbers and yields of weapons, their mode of employment, the meteorological conditions and the existence (or non-existence) of protective measures. The conclusions which may be drawn from the outcome of these studies is, however, that nuclear weapons must never be used.

In these studies various scenarios have been described. They are generally of two kinds: either a counterforce or counter-value strike is assumed. A counterforce strike is aimed at destroying the opponent's missile silos, strategic bomber and submarine bases, aircraft carriers and, to the extent that their positions are known, the strategic submarines at sea. Important military command, communication and surveillance centres might also be included on the target list. In counter-value scenarios, industrial and population centres are assumed to be directly attacked in an attempt to cause unacceptable destruction to the opponent's industrial and human resources. Military facilities might then be targeted or not, depending on the situation.

These studies often neglect consequences other than direct physical damage to human and material resources, such as the effect of the elimination of key industrial sectors in a counter-value attack on the capacity of other industrial production, consequences of loss of transportation facilities and food shortage due to reduction in livestock and crop caused by early fallout radiation and to processing and distribution failures. Food shortage in turn would have consequences on the efficiency of reconstruction labour, the general health of the survivors, the ability to recover for those injured, etc.

Even more difficult to predict, and hence largely omitted in these studies, are the psychological, social and political consequences of the enormous strains imposed on a society which has been subjected to a large-scale nuclear attack. Demoralization of the surviving population may well occur, and could result in erratic, non-social behaviour, aggressiveness or apathy. Disorientation, fear, doubt and antipathy against authorities could occur when strains on a population were severe. Conflicting loyalties with respect to family and to society would add to the staggering organizational problems in an attacked region. Conflicts that exist even in peacetime between ethnic, racial and religious groups, and possibly even political factions within certain countries, could come out in the open following the deprivations, stresses and disorganization of the post-attack period. Political, legal and monetary institutions would, if they survive, most likely be severely weakened and it is in doubt whether an organized central control could be maintained.

The counterforce attack

In a counterforce attack, surface bursts would probably be used in large numbers, as they maximize the probability of destroying hard military targets, e.g., ICBM silos. The major collateral damage would then be caused by early fallout (cf. Fig. XI). Attacks against strategic bomber bases and strategic submarine bases might use air bursts, and, to the extent that these facilities were located close to population centres, blast and thermal effects would cause considerable collateral damage in such areas.

The Office of Technology Assessment study published in 1979 quotes United States Government studies indicating that between 2 million and 20 million Americans would be killed within 30 days after a counter-silo attack on the United States ICBM sites. Another recent study[20] states that in a counterforce attack on the United States, 8 to 12 million fatalities would result if the attack occurred without warning and 5 to 8 million fatalities if there

Figure XI. Risk Areas and Fallout Patterns for Attack vs. Counterforce (Representative March Winds)

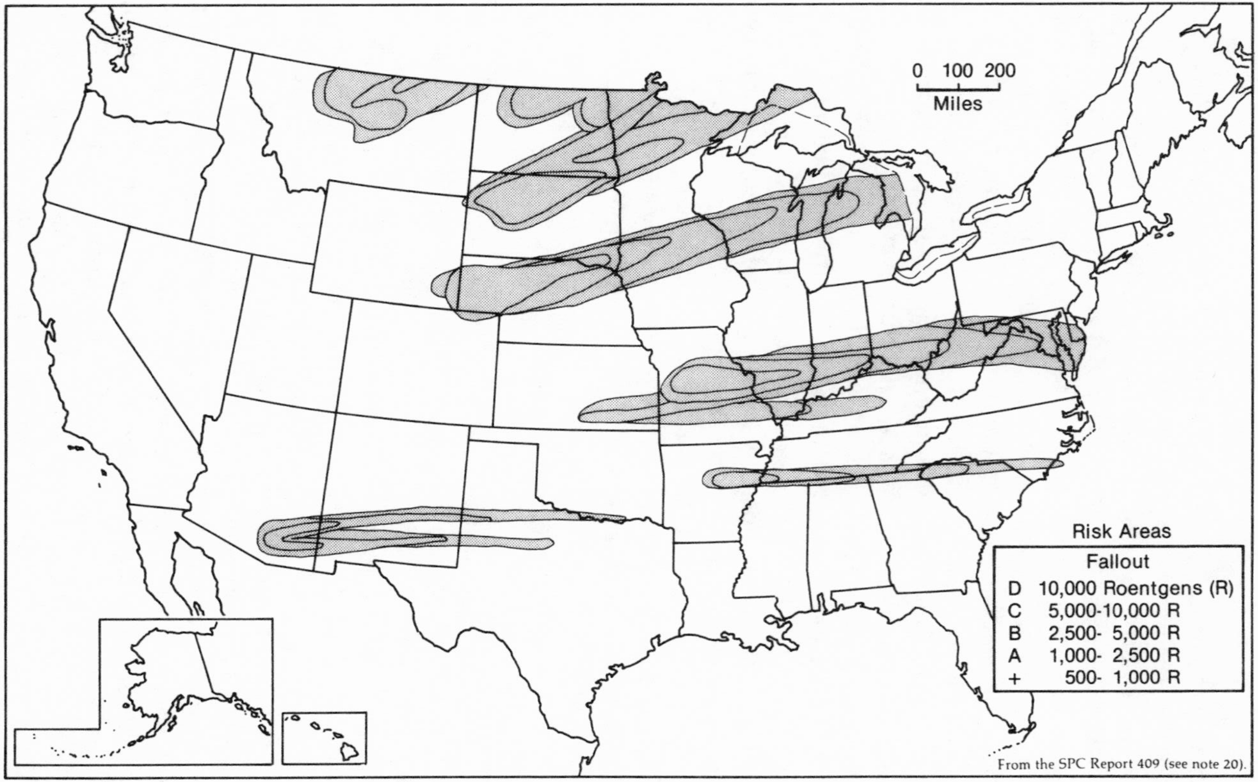
0 100 200
Miles
Risk Areas
Fallout
D 10,000 Roentgens (R)
C 5,000-10,000 R
B 2,500- 5,000 R
A 1,000- 2,500 R
+ 500- 1,000 R

From the SPC Report 409 (see note 20).

were warning. The OTA study concludes that a comprehensive counterforce attack on the United States would produce about 14 million dead even if the present fallout shelter capability were utilized. According to the same source, a United States counterforce strike against the USSR would result in somewhat similar numbers of casualties, i.e., from 2 million to 10 million people killed in a counter-silo strike and 2 million to 13 million in a full counterforce strike. The majority of fatalities within 30 days in a counterforce attack would be caused by radiation due to early fallout from surface bursts.

In the studies referred to above, extensive sheltering of the civilian population is assumed. An uninterrupted stay in shelter during several weeks would be required to avoid still larger casualties. This would cause serious problems of sanitation, food and water supply, air filtration, health, communication to the outer world, psychological tensions, etc. Longer periods of outdoor stay could be considered "safe under the circumstances" after these first weeks, but even after 2 to 3 months the radiation levels would still be far higher than "safe" peacetime levels.

Assuming a "pure" counterforce strike, most productive resources would survive with little material damage. Yet, for some time the economic life would be expected to have collapsed due to the heavy casualties from fallout and other weapon effects and due to fear that still another attack might be imminent. The fact that there might be little material damage to the civilian society would not mean that there would be little economic disturbance. Economic activities, especially in contaminated areas, would be disrupted for months and perhaps years. Long-term damage to the economy would be caused by deaths and long-lasting injuries to the working force, key persons in various organizations, etc. It would take decades before the people killed could be replaced in either the demographic or economic sense.

Radioactive fallout would cause serious problems to agriculture. Livestock would have little protection against fallout. A severe decline in meat supply would therefore result after a certain period of time, and many years would be required to build up new livestock. A considerable decline in the supply of milk, cheese and butter would result. Radiation effects on crops would depend on the season, an attack in spring causing more damage than one in the summer or early autumn. Radioactive elements filtering down into the ground water would be taken up by plants and, through grazing, by cattle and other animals. Quantities of radioactivity could then enter the human system through consumption of crop, meat and milk products from contaminated areas, and this would take its toll through late cancers in the surviving population and genetic defects in future generations.

Public health would be lowered for a long time after the attack, causing extra demands on a nation's medical care facilities. Individuals would be exposed to unknown radiation risks, since enough instruments to measure total radiation received by a person might not be available. Fallout could cause irreversible adverse effects on ecological systems, and genetic mutations changing the ecosystem in unpredictable ways could not be ruled out. Wild animal populations might likewise be considerably affected. But most important, it should be remembered that the attacked country, devastated as it may be, would still have a more than sufficient nuclear capability remaining to deliver a devastating blow to the attacker. This would be according to the logic of deterrence, a counter-value attack.

The counter-value attack

A massive counter-value attack would aim at destroying the very basis of a nation's entire existence by striking at its industrial assets and major urban centres and killing a large fraction of its population. Though military installations might be targeted as well, the destruction of these would not be the primary purpose of this type of attack. The point is rather that a counter-value attack is easier to carry out than a counterforce attack, since less precision is required to strike urban and industrial areas than to destroy missile silos and since the number and size of weapons needed to cause "unacceptable destruction" is less demanding in a counter-value strike. According to former United States Secretary of Defense Robert McNamara, "unacceptable destruction" would require one-fourth to one-third fatalities to a population of a large, industrialized nation and the destruction of half to two thirds of its industrial capacity. According to one report,[21] this was at the time believed to require 400 Mt. equivalent[22] megatonnage in a counter-value attack on the USSR and roughly the same yield in a similar attack on the United States.

In the light of more recent studies, less than 400 equivalent megatons would suffice to cause "unacceptable destruction" of either the USSR or the United States. Thus a number of reports[23] indicate that very heavy damage could be inflicted on either super-Power by relatively few weapons aimed at crucial targets. This is illustrated by table 3. The report[24] from which these tables have been taken also indicates that the nuclear arsenals needed to launch even the heaviest attacks given in the table would be available even after a surprise counterforce attack. In particular, each of the three major types of delivery system (long-range bombers, ICBMs or SLBMs) would retain the number of nuclear weapons necessary to inflict very heavy damage.

With regard to the longer range consequences of a counter-value attack, the larger part of the key industries would have been eliminated. There would therefore be a crucial race between the depletion of remaining supplies of virtually everything and economic recovery under the most adverse conditions. Considering the complexity and interdependence of industrialized society, the shortage of food, energy, transportation, human resources, various machines and vehicles, and complex electronic and electrical systems, and considering as well the disorganization, the human despair and social disruption from starvation, illness and other traumatic experiences, it is obvious that the enormous task of rebuilding society will not be attained within many years—if it ever will.

The national capacity for food production, processing and distribution would be much more severely affected than by a counterforce strike. Destruction of storage facilities, processing plants and transport facilities would result in a general food

Table 3. Vulnerability to counter-value attack
Tables have been adapted from A. Katz, (*op. cit.*). The asymmetry in the data given reflects the different assumptions made: the United States is considered subject to a given (simultaneous) attack. For comparison, the requirement for attacks with similar consequences on the USSR are examined.

Assumed attacks against the United States

Attack number[a]	Total warheads and bombs required	Total megaton equivalents	Total[b] casualties (mill)	Percentage of total industry destroyed
1	300–400	144–166	40–60	25–35
2	400–500	244–266	50–70	35–45
3	500–600	344–366	60–80	45–60
4	700–800	544–566	70–90	60–65

Assumed attacks against the USSR

Attack number	Total population at risk (mill)	Percentage of total industry at risk	Total warheads[c] and bombs required	Total megaton[c] equivalents
1	15[d]	15	26 (181)	26 (25)
2	20	25	90 (300)	90 (40)
3	45	50	144 (631)	144 (86)
4	75	62	303 (1 014)	303 (138)

a. The attacks 1–4 assume 100, 200, 300 and 500 1 Mt. weapons respectively aimed at the 70 largest metropolitan and industrial centres in the United States. To each case another 200–300 weapons of 100 kt. yield have been added.

b. Casualties were estimated from the 1 Mt. weapons only.

c. Numbers outside the parentheses refer to a hypothetical attack with 1 Mt. weapons only, whereas those within parentheses assume an attack with 50 kt. weapons only. Attack No. 4 assumes the 200 largest metropolitan and industrial areas of the USSR to be targeted, and attack No. 1 the 10 largest areas excluding Moscow.

d. Numbers have been rounded to the nearest five.

shortage within a short period of time. This would be likely to continue even after a year or more, as a result of lack of fuel and other energy sources, lack of fertilizers and pesticides and the general destruction or disruption of the infrastructure. Common crop yields in advanced agricultural areas could be reduced by about 50 per cent if no fertilizers and pesticides were available. Radiation hazards and loss of livestock would further aggravate the situation. Malnutrition would in turn affect the general health of the population and impede the reconstruction work. Competition for food would result in starvation and antisocial behaviour.

The destruction of virtually all petroleum capacity, pipeline systems, etc., would have immediate consequences for transportation, heating and electrical power production. Sufficient substitution by coal or natural gas or reconstruction of refineries would take many years. The race between the recovery of industrial output and the depletion of surviving resources would therefore crucially depend on the limited surviving energy supply.

The most demanding immediate medical tasks would be treatment of shock, burn injuries, mechanical injuries and radiation injuries. Many people would suffer from combined injuries. A disproportionately large number of people with medical education would have been killed, since most hospitals are located in urban areas. Lack of sanitation, drugs, antibiotics and modern medical facilities would add to the difficulties, and the food shortage would further degrade the general health conditions.

For the nation as a whole, a most serious problem would be the destruction of many social and political institutions at a time when demands would far exceed the normal capacity of such institutions, had they remained viable. A counter-value attack could well entail the successive decay, if not the sudden collapse, of societal structure.

Global aspects
Environmental effects

The consequences of a major nuclear war would not be restricted to the nuclear-weapon States. Even if there were no

direct nuclear attack against any non-nuclear-weapon State, there
are probable collateral effects from a nuclear war between the
super-Powers. In a longer perspective, fallout radiation after a
large nuclear war would affect the whole world (although pre-
dominantly the hemisphere in which the war was fought). The
same could hold true for some other physical effects influencing
the environment, such as the dispersal of nitrous oxides and dust
in the atmosphere.

Of the world-wide effects associated with nuclear warfare, that
of global fallout is the most thoroughly studied and known. The
different ways in which airborne radioactivity (including tritium
and carbon-14, which are not deposited on the ground) can reach
and irradiate humans have largely been derived from empirically
established fallout intensities produced by atmospheric tests. The
transport of water-borne activity with ocean currents has also
been investigated. These surveys have been supplemented by
laboratory research regarding the effects of ionizing radiations on
living organisms.

The result of this knowledge has been applied to an "unre-
stricted" nuclear war in a number of studies,[25] and the corresponding toll of the world's population over the years (including
future generations) has been estimated. As an example, global
fallout from a total explosive yield of 10,000 Mt., i.e., well over
half of what presently exists in the world's nuclear stockpiles,
would cause of the order of 5 to 10 million additional deaths from
cancer within the next 40 years. In addition, a similar amount of
(non-lethal) thyroid cancers would result. Genetic damage would
appear in about as many instances as lethal cancers, half of which
would be manifest in the following two generations and the rest in
generations thereafter.

Extensive early fallout (i.e., from surface bursts) over nations
not directly involved in a nuclear war may also occur. To quantify estimates of short- and long-term radiation injuries from this
fallout is much more difficult than for global fallout, as they
depend on meteorological conditions and protective measures

taken. Under adverse conditions, cases of late cancers and hereditary defects would run into some millions.

Ionizing radiation could possibly also cause many mutations in
plants and animals. There has been speculation that some of these
mutations might change the ecosystem in unpredictable ways, but
too little is known about the physical and biological processes
involved to make predictions in this field.

A large nuclear war would cause the injection of substantial
quantities of nitrogen oxides into the upper atmosphere, especially if a multitude of explosions in the megaton range were to
occur. These oxides would then reach the ozone layer in the
stratosphere and might, through chemical reactions, partially
destroy it in a few months. A period of about 5 years is believed to
be required to restore the layer again. Since ozone is an effective
barrier to solar ultraviolet radiation, a depletion of the ozone
column would result in an increase of this radiation at the surface
of the earth. Unfortunately, the full biological implications of an
increased ultraviolet radiation to ecosystems at various latitudes
are not known. However, the incidence of skin cancer is thought
to be related to the amount of ultraviolet radiation received.
Mutations in plants and animals might also increase.

The extent to which the release of a given quantity of nitrogen
oxides would deplete the ozone layer is at present not entirely
clear. A 1975 study by the United States National Academy of
Sciences reported a 30 to 70 per cent reduction of the ozone layer
if a total yield of 10,000 Mt. were to be exploded. Later investiga-
tions have led to a better understanding of the chemistry
involved. It is now believed that such a heavy depletion could
occur only if most of the total yield derived from multi-megaton
weapons.

A sizable change of ozone concentration in the stratosphere
would seriously affect stratospheric heating. This in turn would
change temperature conditions in the troposphere and hence
cause possible climatic changes at the earth's surface. Large
amounts of dust injected in the atmosphere might further add to

these changes. It has been estimated that 10,000 Mt. would pollute the stratosphere with 10^7-10^8 tons of material, i.e., of the same order as that injected by the eruption of Krakatoa.[26] Climatic changes would be expected to be smaller in tropical and subtropical zones and larger at higher latitudes. In the latter regions, however, even small changes, such as a cooling of 1° C., would have serious consequences. (It is estimated that the Krakatoa event at most caused a temperature reduction of 0.5° C. over a few years.) The 1° C. cooling could severely hamper wheat growing in Canada and parts of the USSR, for instance, due to a reduction of the number of frost-free days. Although the recovery time associated with possible global climatic changes due to a large nuclear war would probably be only a few years, present knowledge is insufficient to definitely rule out more persistent effects.

Social, economic and political effects

Whereas many physical and biological effects of nuclear war can be identified and to some extent investigated, the world-wide economic and social disruption that would be an unavoidable consequence of a large nuclear war is more difficult to examine. Today's world is characterized by a large and increasing international interdependency. A substantial number of important products are made up of parts and components from all over the world. Financially, the business activities in various countries are highly interrelated through agreements as well as flows of currencies and credits. And the nuclear Powers are also the major nodes in this international network of trade.

To describe coherently even the main effects of a large nuclear war on the economic and social world situation is not possible. In this context it seems particularly prudent to quote the Office of Technology Assessment report mentioned previously: "The effects of a nuclear war that cannot be calculated are at least as important as those for which calculations are attempted." Some general ideas could be inferred from the study of past wars as well as of peacetime crises; examples in the latter category would include the collapse of the United States stock market in 1929, but also recent distress situations such as those following the widespread crop failures in 1972 and 1974. However, historical evidence dwindles beside the possible aftermath of a large nuclear war.

An analysis of the consequences for world trade in general and supply of essential commodities in particular would have to take into account both decreasing production volumes and the possible breakdown of the organization of world commerce and communications. When there are serious problems in both these respects, they would soon have an impact on everyday conditions for most people on the globe.

Most critical would be the world food supply: in many developing countries, famine is an ever-present threat even under stable and peaceful conditions, and a large and continuous international grains trade is needed to prevent starvation.[27] In addition, modern agriculture increasingly uses inputs from many different branches of industry. Among these are various kinds of tools and machinery as well as pesticides and herbicides, but above all fertilizers from the chemical industry which—together with energy—are required continuously and are absolutely necessary if land resources are limited.

The world food situation some time after the war could be crudely assessed by recalling that wheat is the most important grain—and consequently foodstuff—in international trade. The importance of the North American exports is well known. During 1979, for instance, the United States alone exported about 37 million tons of wheat, which is almost half the world trade in wheat. In addition the United States and Canada have about 40 million tons of the wheat stocks and if they were unavailable after a nuclear war the world food situation would become disastrous in a very short time. This could mean that famine would spread to hundreds of millions of people.

The major cause of hunger today is poverty—the lack of resources with which to buy enough food or enough fertilizers, fuels, machinery, etc., for an adequate indigenous production. This would be even more pronounced after a large nuclear war. As exports are necessary to pay for imports, the loss of substantial export markets—detrimental to most nations—would be disastrous for the poor, food-importing countries, and there would be severe disruptions of this kind if the United States and the USSR were devastated to an extent that eliminated them as partners in trade for even a couple of years.

The United States is one of the largest trading countries in the world. Very few countries have less than 10 per cent of their export market in the United States, and some have between 50 per cent and 70 per cent of their export destined to the United States. Likewise, the United States is the largest single contributor both to development aid and to international organizations like the United Nations. The foreign trade of the Soviet Union is about one third of that of the United States, and about half of all Soviet trade is within the Council for Mutual Economic Assistance (CMEA). For the East European countries, a loss of the USSR as a trading partner would be a disaster, as the USSR takes 33 per cent of their total export. The CMEA economies are also highly co-ordinated with the Soviet economy. Some non-CMEA nations have from 20 to 40 per cent of their export market in the USSR, and there are also a number of countries very heavily dependent on Soviet development assistance.

All countries in the world would suffer a drastic reduction of foreign trade, entailing difficulties and economic losses. There are interactive effects of different kinds:

(a) Eliminated countries may be major suppliers of exclusive manufacturers of many technology-intensive products and ser-vices;
(b) Export items are inputs in other countries' export products;
(c) Downgraded foreign trade might cause shortages of essen-tial equipment, semi-manufactures, spare parts, etc., which no longer could be paid for, thereby reducing the domestic output;
(d) Decreased income *per capita* and increased unemployment would result in redistribution of consumption patterns and hence of demand, supply and production in many countries.

The annihilation of the major financial and trading centres of the world, such as New York, London, Moscow and other such cities, would inevitably lead to the destruction of the elaborate system of international finance and trade as it is now constituted, thus eliminating the orderly transfer of goods and services that characterize international economic relations.

Globally, the physical means of transport and communication would probably not be too severely affected. When properly organized after the initial confusion, remaining resources for shipping, land and air transport and telecommunications would prove adequate for the reduced post-war world trade, possibly even if some kind of international relief programmes were instituted. By securing spare parts through "cannibalism", it should be possible to keep even advanced aircraft functioning for several years. All this is under the assumption that oil (and other energy resources) were available. However, the physical consequences of the war do not include an additional deficit of oil in the world as a whole, as the United States imports oil while the USSR is currently slightly more than self-sustaining.

In the general hardship and unrest that would follow a nuclear war, countries with a grain surplus might not act for the benefit of starving people in distant countries. Their surplus might instead be used, for example, for bilateral bartering for raw materials. In a somewhat longer perspective, the fertilizer situation would be a serious problem, as the United States and the USSR are major producers of fertilizers. Even though most of their production is for domestic consumption, the unavailability of large quantities of essential agricultural inputs would be a more severe problem than the loss of grain surplus nations, because it would threaten the capability of all fertilizer importers to produce food.

If almost all major nations in Europe were impaired or eliminated in addition to the United States and the USSR, an analysis of the consequences on world affairs sounds euphemistic, as there would probably be very little business to transact, at least between these regions and the rest of the world. The economic importance of these countries to the world community stands out by noting that together they could account for between half and two thirds of the world's gross national product and trade.

A major difference in comparison with the previous scenario is the impossibility of heavy relief programmes for the devastated countries, as the surviving industrialized countries would not possess the capability for such a task. This would be an aggravating circumstance which could rule out any chance of international economic recovery for a long time. Furthermore, many of the non-belligerents would be developing countries which were suppliers of raw materials and agricultural products of less immediate importance after a large nuclear war. These might expect an almost total cessation of foreign trade.

In addition to this, there would probably be a total breakdown in the multilateral system of payments and in the United Nations and World Bank organizations. Important sections and main stations of the international telecommunications system via cable and satellite would also be out of order along with major urban areas in Europe.

Food would be in very short supply, especially after some time when the shortages of fertilizers had reduced the yield in most parts of the world. These fertilizer shortages would be much more severe in this scenario. The result might well be that hundreds of millions would starve to death. The global disaster would be further aggravated by the scarcity of transport equipment, pharmaceuticals and pesticides, which would increase the horror and the plagues.

All surviving countries trying to switch over their domestic production to an increased level of self-sufficiency would have to accomplish this change in a race with time before stocks ran out completely. A failure to achieve viability (i.e., production at least equalling consumption plus depreciation) would result in many additional deaths and much additional economic, political and social deterioration. Thus a downward self-feeding spiral might start. Which way the economy in a particular region or country would go is unpredictable, however.

The discussion above has focused on a few quantifiable items. It must be borne in mind, however, that there are innumerable other aspects to be investigated, some of an intangible nature and all interactive. A local war or threat of war in any region might divert industry and materials into producing for the war effort and away from the economy and standard of living. A breakdown of law and order in some regions of the world might severely hamper the recuperation of international trade. Tremendous importance must also be attached to the political and social institutions affecting both the motivation of individuals and the overall efficiency with which a nation's human, financial and natural resources would be used in agricultural production and the way the food would be distributed.

The motivation of people to come to grips with the huge and seemingly hopeless task of rebuilding a world destroyed would perhaps be the decisive factor in some cases. One should have no high expectations in this regard, if the cultural, social and political values which are today the driving forces behind a great deal of evolution suddenly lost their meaning.

In fact, there is very little reason to believe that the political and social situation in any country would be unchanged after a large nuclear war. Many nations among those we know would probably disappear. Others might be virtually depopulated by famine and mass migration. The system of international security would have been destroyed, and so would to a large extent the traditional pattern of those States, nations and societies which might survive.

Effects of nuclear testing

As was indicated in chapter III, the nuclear Powers have performed in all more than 1,200 nuclear tests. In the absence of officially given numbers, the figures quoted in table 4 are estimates based on the data available. As seen from the table, the majority of tests have been and still are conducted by the United States and the USSR. In recent years, an average of 30 to 40 tests have been carried out annually. Nearly all of them are underground tests, as nuclear testing in other environments is forbidden by the partial test-ban Treaty of 1963, which has been adhered to by the United

States, the USSR and the United Kingdom. The two other
nuclear-weapon States, France and China, are not parties to the
Treaty. China is still conducting atmospheric tests, whereas
France declared in 1974 that it would abandon testing in the
atmosphere. Nearly all tests are carried out at special test sites,
some of them outside the territory of the testing State (see map in
Fig. XII).

Table 4. Known and presumed nuclear explosions up to
31 December 1979

A = Atmospheric   U = Underground   T = Total

Nation	16 July 1945– 4 August 1963			5 August 1963– 31 December 1979			Total		
	A	U	T	A	U	T	A	U	T
United States of America	193	110[a]	303	—	362	362	193	472	665
USSR	161	3	163	—	262	262	161	265	426
United Kingdom	21	2	23	—	7	7	21	9	30
France	4	4	8	41	37	78	45	41	86
China	—	—	—	21	4	25	21	4	25
India	—	—	—	0	1	1	0	1	1
TOTAL	379	119	498	62	673	735	441	792	1 233

Sources: SIPRI Yearbook 1980
Zander and Araskog: Nuclear explosions, 1945–1972. Basic Data. FOA 4
Report A 4505–A1, Research Institute of National Defense, Stockholm, April
1973, with later amendments.

a. Some of these may have taken place after 5 August 1963.

The main direct harm to the world population from nuclear-
weapon tests derives from the world-wide dispersion of radioactive matter occurring in particular after atmospheric tests. The
source of the radioactivity, which does not differ from that generated by nuclear explosions in a war, is the fission products, as
well as many other nuclides produced at the time of explosion in
the nuclear device itself, in other structural materials and in the
close surroundings of the explosion point. After the debris

reaches ground level and enters the biosphere there are different pathways for the individual radio-nuclides to deliver radiation to man.

The United Nations Scientific Committee on the Effects of Atomic Radiation continuously estimates the doses that have been delivered, and will be delivered in the future, from all nuclear tests performed. In its 1977 report to the General Assembly,[28] the Committee summarized the doses committed by all nuclear tests carried out before 1976. These are estimated to have caused a global dispersion of radioactive debris from about 145 Mt. of fission yield. Part of the radiation received by man is external, coming from debris deposited on the ground. Important doses to different organs of the body also come from several radio-nuclides (notably strontium-90 and cesium-137) which enter man via food or through inhalation, and act as internal sources of radiation during their combined physical and biological lifespan.

The radiation doses averaged over the world population from external and internal sources are estimated to be roughly equal, the total whole-body dose (up to the year 2000) being about 120 millirad.[29] This means that past nuclear tests which have contaminated the biosphere have committed of the order of 1 millirad per Mt. fission averaged over the world population. To quantify this in terms of possible cancer deaths and serious hereditary ill health one can use the uncertain but commonly cited estimate of 2 to 3 deaths due to cancer or genetic damage for each 10,000 manrad collective dose. For the world population this would lead to one death for each kiloton fission exploded. With this measure all past atmospheric tests could be equivalent to about 150,000 premature deaths world-wide, and approximately 90 per cent of these would be expected to occur in the Northern Hemisphere. However, it should be noted not only that this figure is based on an estimate of the risks associated with low radiation doses which in itself is a matter of scientific controversy, but also that even if that estimate is correct, there is no way of identifying these cases among the many millions of other cancer deaths during the same period of time.

When a nuclear device detonates underground an almost spherical cavity is formed and at somewhat larger distances the rock is cracked. The radius of the crack zone depends on the explosion yield and the properties of the surrounding rock, but is of the order of a few hundred metres. At larger distances the only effects of a fully contained underground nuclear explosion are the outgoing seismic waves. Close to an explosion, these signals can be quite strong but they decrease rapidly with increasing distance from the explosion point. Even from large explosions, seismic signals at great distances are smaller than those generated by earthquakes occuring several times a week in various parts of the world. Thus, there is no evidence that underground nuclear explosions have initiated any earthquakes in areas at great distances from the explosion point. Neither is there any physical process suggested by which such triggering could be possible. The seismic effects of underground nuclear explosions are confined to a fairly limited area around the explosion point, and there is no evidence that such explosions could generate secondary events in other areas.

If an underground nuclear explosion takes place comparatively close to the surface, the explosion might break through the surface and release some of the radioactive fission products into the atmosphere. A few cases of such "venting", of such a magnitude that it could be detected outside the borders of the country where the test was conducted, did occur during the first years of underground testing. Underground test explosions in later years seem to have been contained to a higher degree, although of course any leak would contribute slightly to the total radioactive contamination of the biosphere.

Civil defence

A number of nations have organized a civil defence to meet the demands of a conventional war, with or without additional features specifically designed for nuclear war situations. Traditionally, civil defence comprises measures to avoid civilian casualties, like sheltering, warning and evacuation to limit immediate damage, and firefighting and rescue efforts to give immediate relief to the injured and homeless.

Some of these measures could help to limit the number of fatalities caused by a nuclear attack. In view of the large devastation caused, especially if nuclear weapons are used directly against the population, available resources for post-attack relief could prove totally inadequate, however. What matters most then is the potential for long-term survival, recovery and reconstruction. These long-term aspects would become particularly important after large attacks, when the survival of the entire population would be in jeopardy. For this reason, traditional civil defence should be discussed in conjunction with other measures designed to allow or facilitate national recovery after a nuclear war.

Civil defence is sometimes regarded between the super-Powers as a component of the strategic balance and it is then even maintained that a strong civil defence effort could upset that balance. This seems to be an exaggeration of current civil defence capabilities, as in our time no civil defence system could provide reliable protection for most of the citizenry under all circumstances. The possible value depends largely on the attack scenario. Civil defence could, for instance, be very effective in saving lives which would otherwise be lost to fallout in a limited attack against hard targets. On the other hand, it would be far less effective in a war involving strikes against industry in cities, or against the civilian population as such. This holds true for non-nuclear-weapon States as well as nuclear-weapon States in a nuclear war. Even in countries which do not themselves come under nuclear attack, civil defence would be needed to deal with fallout from large numbers of nuclear explosions in neighbouring countries.

Civil defence methods

The two means most commonly considered for protecting the population from nuclear-weapon effects are evacuation and sheltering. Evacuation of population from areas expected to come under attack has to be planned very carefully in advance. Apart from transportation and housing of evacuees, this planning must include at least short-term provisions for the relocated population. Information and instructions to the general public would have to be issued in advance. Even if instructions were available, however, the execution of an evacuation would probably be accompanied by confusion and panic. Large-scale evacuation is therefore, in most cases, no attractive option.

To start an evacuation too early would mean an unnecessary disruption of everyday activities; to start too late would worsen the prospects for those evacuated, as their vulnerability would be highest during the transfer phase. The very fact that an evacuation had started might even precipitate the attack, and there is also the possibility of targeting the relocated population. These constraints are valid in any type of war, but in a nuclear war they would be more severe. In addition, there is the particular problem of radioactive fallout, as available radiation shielding can generally be expected to be inferior in rural areas. Furthermore, the location of serious fallout areas cannot be predicted in advance.

Sheltering, which is a very expensive protective measure, implies hardening against nuclear-weapon effects rather than avoiding them. In nuclear war, shelters would have to protect against ionizing radiation as well as blast, collapsing buildings and flying debris, thermal radiation and fire. Shelters that offer reasonable protection against mechanical loads would, generally speaking, give adequate radiation shielding. Special shelter design features would be necessary, however, to deal with the extended air blast of nuclear weapons. Difficult problems would also be the long-lasting thermal load on a shelter buried under a large heap of smouldering rubble and the ventilation of the shelter under these conditions. Filtration of the incoming air would be desirable to keep out radioactive dust and toxic gases. Ordinary filters do not, however, remove the carbon monoxide generated by smouldering fires.

Food, water and sanitation would have to be available as people might have to stay in shelter for a long time after a nuclear attack to avoid the effects of fallout radiation or because rescue work was seriously impeded. Under heavy fallout conditions, as would prevail for instance about 30 km. downwind of a 1 Mt. fission surface burst, people could leave their shelters after two days, provided that they could leave the contaminated area immediately and be outside it in an hour or two. If such evacuation were not possible and they had to remain on the spot for a couple of days, they would have to stay in shelters for a month, if acute radiation injuries were to be avoided. One hundred km downwind, the corresponding times would be a few hours and a week, respectively. In both these instances, there would be a high incidence of late radiation cancers among the survivors, even if the proper sheltering periods could be observed.

Rescue efforts in a nuclear war would pose special problems because of the enormity of the operation involved and because of the possible existence of residual radiation. There would be many fires to extinguish and large masses of debris from collapsed buildings to remove. It would not be possible to assign such resources that all survivors trapped in shelters or basements could be saved, even if sophisticated disaster plans had been prepared in advance.

The presence of fallout would necessitate equipment and routines for surveying the contaminated area and monitoring the radiation. There would be a large need of fallout shelters which, however, could be produced more easily and more cheaply than blast shelters. Even in non-belligerent countries, problems might be posed by fallout from explosions elsewhere in the world. After megaton surface bursts and in unfavourable weather conditions, outdoor doses large enough to cause acute radiation injuries could occur up to about 1,000 km. from the targeted areas.

Long-term survival and recovery

After a nuclear attack (and to some extent after fallout contamination originating from an attack elsewhere) domestic production and distribution of various commodities would be disturbed and international trade disrupted. Among the most important factors would be those related to food, energy, medical supplies, clothing and provisional housing. Crisis stockpiling of basic supplies would be an important precaution for dealing with these difficulties during the first days of weeks. However, distribution problems could quickly become critical.

The most urgent problem would be to ensure the continuous production of food. This production may have to be independent of imported goods, which could cause particular difficulties in countries where agriculture was highly mechanized. Fallout would have taken a toll of the livestock, partly because of difficulties to tend the animals properly and partly as a consequence of radiation injuries to them. An additional difficulty would be that some farmland and pastures might have been rendered useless for years due to radioactive contamination.

The super-Powers have reportedly held discussions at the national level regarding systematic protection of the industrial base through hardening and dispersion. Hardening would mean protection of the buildings and machines up to a certain level of overpressure. Significant increase in hardness is particularly difficult for some industries, such as oil refineries. Dispersion is more expensive and could evidently come about only as a result of long-range planning. It is doubtful whether any such effort is worthwhile. The hardening of a targeted industry could be countered by detonating weapons at lower altitudes or by increasing weapon accuracy. Similarly, dispersion could be rendered insufficient by new developments in numbers of warheads and weapons accuracy. No country is known to have attempted significant hardening or dispersion of industry.

In endeavouring to reconstruct both agriculture and other basic industry, the overriding problem would be to reach a production rate at least equal to a minimum consumption rate before stockpiles were entirely depleted. However, the organized effort necessary to master this awesome task would require an unequalled level of determination and insight among both the population and the leadership.

Existing and potential civil defence programmes

A complete civil defence programme consists of a number of components which have to operate together. There are doubts, however, concerning the effectiveness of even a well-balanced and largely implemented complete system in a nuclear war. This is due partly to the basic uncertainties concerning characteristics of the attack, behaviour of the population, object response to weapons effects, influence of weather, climatic conditions, etc., and partly to the enormous force of nuclear weapons, which allows the attacker to neutralize the effect of any civil defence effort simply by employing a few more, and somewhat larger, nuclear weapons. Unless it was presumed that the attacker's objective was to kill as many civilians as possible, however, civil defence could help substantially to lessen the consequences of an attack and to ameliorate conditions after it. Thus, civil defence is warranted by humanitarian concern, notwithstanding the doubts of its capacity to deal with all situations.

To estimate the actual cost of various national civil defence efforts is very difficult. Costs are calculated and accounted for differently in different countries. Furthermore, comparisons between differently composed programmes may be misleading, particularly as all programmes are not solely or primarily nuclear-oriented. The examples given in table 5 should be examined with these qualifications in mind.

Table 5. Some examples of annual civil defense costs

Nation	Approximate costs per capita (US dollars)
Switzerland ⎫ Norway ⎬ Israel ⎭	more than 10
Sweden	9[a]
USSR	8[b]
Finland ⎫ Denmark ⎭	4
Federal Republic of Germany	3.5
Netherlands	2.5
United States	0.5[c]

Source: DCPA *Information Bulletin*, 5 April 1979, No. 303.

a. Amount quoted covers traditional civil defense, including radiological defense, but no crisis stockpiling.

b. Amount quoted covers personnel costs, shelter construction and operation of some military installations of civil defence importance. See also Soviet Civil Defense, the Department of State, United States of America, Special Report No. 47, September 1978.

c. Mainly administration and planning for protection against nuclear effects.

There are, however, two additional and more important caveats to be remembered. One is that very little is or even could be known about the actual value of existing civil defence programmes in a large nuclear war, as fortunately they have not yet been tested. The other is that there are a large number of nations in the world which cannot afford to spend anything at all on civil defence, even if they were convinced of the favourable cost-effectiveness ratio of the various measures necessary.

Figure XII. Test Sites 1945–1979

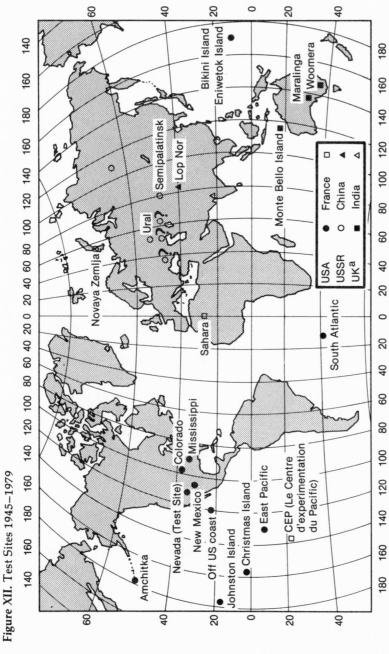

No nuclear explosions have been conducted in Australia since 1957. The Australian government is opposed to all testing of nuclear explosive devices.

107

V

The Doctrines of Deterrence and Other Theories Concerning Nuclear Weapons

Doctrines and nuclear weapons

LONG BEFORE THE EMERGENCE of nuclear weapons, military doctrines of various kinds have been used to describe the intended conduct of future wars, to control or guide the use of force and to determine the conditions thereof. The existence of nuclear weapons and the rapid technological development in this field during the last 30 years have given rise to numerous military doctrines relating to the use or threat of use of nuclear weapons and led to their constant revision.

The concept of military doctrine is used in somewhat different ways by the major military Powers. In the West military doctrines tend to be regarded as operational concepts whose postulates are confined to the use or threat of use of force. Thus, most strategic doctrines in the West deal with policies concerning the use of nuclear weapons. In the Soviet Union military doctrine has a broader meaning and has been defined as "an officially accepted system of views in a given State and in its armed forces on the nature of war and methods of conducting it and on preparation of the country and army for war".[30] The Soviet view of military science embraces the entire range of political, economic and technological considerations which might affect the course of a war.

Military doctrines are often formally expressed in statements and speeches by national leaders and ranking military personalities, but they are also reflected in the military preparations of a given State or group of States, e.g., in decisions on procurement and deployment, in training manuals, as well as in military and political periodicals and books.

A large spectrum of thinking exists on the subject of nuclear weapons and their possible use. This thinking is sometimes grouped into certain "schools", depending on the attitude towards the use of nuclear weapons and the role of these weapons in international relations. These schools range from total acceptance, through scepticism and relativism, to total rejection of nuclear weapons. Most notably, the theories that consider use of nuclear weapons as an integral element of the security of States are hard to reconcile with the ideas behind the United Nations Charter, sometimes referred to as the concept of "peace through law". This will be further discussed in chapter VII.

When evaluating the means and importance of military doctrines, consideration must be given to the fact that a given doctrine or doctrinal statement may serve different political and military purposes. Even if a particular doctrine has the form of operational concepts for the conduct of war, its objective may also be to serve as a political declaration with relevance for a situation of peace. Its main target can be a potential military adversary, its ally or a group of States allied to it, or even political and military circles in one's own State. Examples of this are the doctrines of nuclear deterrence, by which the super-Powers try to convince each other that it is meaningless to use nuclear weapons against each other.

The credibility of a certain doctrine is naturally dependent upon the means to implement it. Although any doctrine can be openly professed, to be credible a State must have at its disposal the military means which would correspond to the doctrine. A State must also display that it has the will, if need be, to implement it.

Nuclear weapons and deterrence

The phenomenon of deterrence probably existed already at very early stages of human existence. It is based essentially on the threat of use of force to prevent someone from carrying out his intentions. It can take the form of either a threat to inflict severe consequences in case a certain act is carried out (deterrence by punishment), or of a threat to prevent by force the actual implementation of the act (deterrence by denial). The principle of deterrence has in all times served as a basis for military doctrines for the defence of States. In the nuclear age, however, the meaning of deterrence has acquired totally new dimensions.

Nuclear deterrence in present conditions is different from deterrence with conventional weapons in several ways: it can be immediate, total and global. Never before have States been able to inflict upon each other almost instant punishment. In the nuclear age it is possible to carry out an attack in a matter of hours, even minutes. Never before have States been able to destroy the very basis for continued existence of other States and regions. And never before has it been possible to carry out such destruction on any part of the globe, no matter how distant.

A State's defensive capability has in the past often been the basis for the practice of deterrence, on the principle of making the outcome of aggression more costly than the benefits which an adversary could derive from it. In the nuclear age, however, the very cornerstone of what is projected as defence is offensive capability, while defensive capabilities—in the true sense of the word— are very limited. Thus, deterrence can be said to be based fundamentally on offensive capability, meaning the ability to inflict intolerable damage on the adversary. This holds true also in a situation where deterrence by denial, e.g., by the threat of use of tactical nuclear weapons in a limited battlefield conflict situation, is considered, as this involves a risk of escalation to higher levels of nuclear engagement and thus in itself from the beginning carries an element of deterrence by punishment, which always risks becoming the dominating feature.

The above does not mean that defence capabilities today are absolutely non-existent. A technological breakthrough in defence systems is unlikely but cannot be totally excluded. Besides, ABM defence capabilities are limited by the Treaty concluded under the terms of the first SALT agreement of 1972 and of the Protocol to that Treaty signed in Moscow in 1974. The ABM Treaty indicated that both super-Powers were prepared to continue to rely on the concept of deterrence as a basic feature of their strategic relationship. Concluding this Treaty, they both implicitly acknowledged the fact that their respective high value targets must remain hostage in case of aggression by the other.

The concept of deterrence implies that beyond a certain level of expected damage, States will prefer peace to war. In the mid-1960s, former United States Secretary of Defense Robert McNamara stated that unacceptable destruction would require one fourth to one third fatalities to a population of a large, industrialized nation and destruction of half to two thirds of the entire industrial capacity. Likewise, Mr. McNamara has illustrated the United States' capacity for "assured destruction" by stating that the United States, even after suffering a first strike, could then in a second strike have destroyed two fifths of the Soviet Union's population and 70 per cent of its industry.

The notion of a deterring level of destruction, it should be recognized, is entirely relative, for reasons of geographical differences, demographic considerations (dispersion or concentration of the population) and other factors (including historical traditions and experiences). It would most certainly be different for different States. The notion of "minimum deterrence" is therefore difficult to define since no one can define with certainty what constitutes intolerable reprisal. In any case, the order of damage likely in a nuclear conflict is beyond all historical experience.

Moreover, it is probable that States make different assessments of the relationship between stakes and risk. While the risk depends on the cost of attack, on the one hand, and the reprisals or punishment which it will invite on the other, the assessment by a potential attacking State will also depend on the importance it attaches to what it might gain. A traditional view has been that the more desirable the stakes, the more inclined the challenging State will be to take risks. In a conflict situation between two nuclear-weapon States, however, the risks are so high that many find it difficult to see what gains could possibly make up for the level of destruction by a reprisal. This raises the fundamental issue as to whether there are any stakes which may justify risking a nuclear war.

The realization of the enormous risk levels inherent in deterrence with nuclear weapons on the one hand, and the evolution and diversification of nuclear weapons on the other hand, were the essential factors leading to the introduction of the theory of flexible response. Accordingly, depending on the seriousness of the situation, a State may respond to an attack with what it regards as appropriate means, which may be conventional weapons, tactical nuclear weapons, or various modes of employment of strategic nuclear weapons. Thus an effort would be made to preserve as wide as possible a range of means in order to avoid having to choose between "all or nothing". It is in this context that deterrence by denial has become a more frequently mentioned option. As has already been pointed out, however, the risk of escalation makes every option based on nuclear deterrence by denial an extremely risky venture.

Doctrines of nuclear deterrence have been criticized not only for involving unacceptably high risks and holding populations hostage, but also for treating the conduct of nuclear war as if computers rather than human beings were in decision-making positions, for building upon an inherently unstable balance and, last but not least, for the lack of acceptable solutions in case of failure of deterrence.

Very sophisticated doctrines of deterrence have been questioned with reference to their relation to reality. A prerequisite for their effectiveness has been said to be that their main features must be mutually understood by the States concerned and that decision-makers and actors should act rationally. Although the concept of deterrence lies at the basis of the relationship between the super-Powers, it is difficult to state with any degree of certainty whether they have accepted the existence of each other's doctrines and whether there exists a mutual understanding of the basic concepts. Some analysts even say that the doctrine professed by one side might dialectically produce the opposite doctrine on the other side.[31] It is evident that the two super-Powers follow each other's strategic thinking with the closest attention.

It has often been questioned whether decision-makers and others involved in a situation which subjects people to the extremely heavy stress that decisions on the conduct of a nuclear war would most likely produce, would act efficiently and according to the predetermined rules of a doctrine. Experience from various fields of human activity, especially in conducting war, points to the possibility that mistakes are often committed and that behavior not infrequently tends to be erratic in such circumstances.

Peace resting on the system of deterrence has been said to require approximate parity or balance between the forces of the States involved. The view is held that parity ceases to exist if one side acquires a "first-strike capability", i.e., the capacity to deliver a nuclear strike against the other without risking an intolerable reprisal. In these conditions, the general fear is that deterrence can or may fail. Yet the concept of parity rests on a situation which is inherently difficult to evaluate. Each super-Power's nuclear arsenal consists of many components of different size, function and importance. Since each of these components may be subject to constant technological development on both sides, but not always simultaneously, parity is a process whose equilibrium must continuously be re-established. Hence, the notion of balance is then, by definition, almost unstable. In addition, one cannot ignore the psychological factors in the assessment of mutual destruction capabilities. The problems connected with establishing parity are illustrated by the introduction of the broader concept of "essential equivalence", which allows for asymmetries in the respective strategic arsenals.

Perhaps the most severe criticism which could be addressed towards a system of security based on the concept of nuclear deterrence relates to the problem of what happens if deterrence fails. It is argued that deterrence has thus far prevented a world conflict, and consequently that deterrence has worked. Apart from the fact that many other factors of a historical, political and other nature have to be considered in that context, it is a truism to say that deterrence works, because that statement will hold true only until history disproves it. At the doctrinal level, the idea of intra-war deterrence has been introduced both through the concept of flexible response and through the "selective targeting options" concept which is currently being professed by one State. At the same time, some observers state that war-fighting is an important component of the doctrinal bases for nuclear arsenals of some States. Perhaps the most dramatic question is the risk of a nuclear war which could be launched by accident, either because of technical failure or human error. At this particular level, while the nuclear-weapon States have no doubt set up control and command systems which are designed to minimize these risks, the possibility of the accidental launch of one or many nuclear weapons, however small the probability of such risks, cannot be totally excluded altogether.

History indicates that once a particular type of weapon has been developed past the testing stage it will generally be used. This has not been true of nuclear weapons, with one exception, but there can be no assurance that it will remain so. Thus, the doctrine of nuclear deterrence remains open to the criticism that, given the nature of these weapons, the risks of the failure of deterrence are correspondingly higher. It may be argued that they are too high to be worth taking. In these circumstances, some States prefer to base their security on the rather hazardous concept of the balance of terror, maintaining that the urgent priority is to make it as stable as possible. The majority of international society believes, however, that this is illusory, in terms of securing a permanent and secure system of world peace.

Doctrines and technological development

The strategic principles underlying the threat of possible use of nuclear weapons may be regarded as having become increasingly sophisticated as the range of means available for implementing this threat has become wider, more complex and more diversified. This does not mean that military doctrines have no effect on the development of different types of weapon systems. The doctrines form a theoretical complex that serves as a basis for defence policy and, consequently, for the actual deployment of military forces, with all the research, development and manufacture of new weapons that this implies. On the whole, however, it is the technological development that has promoted a readjustment of military doctrines rather than the doctrines that have prompted the development of the different weapons systems now possessed by the major military Powers.

As long as deterrence between the super-Powers remains linked to the concept of populations held mutually hostage, it is obvious that the introduction of any new technology that may be perceived as potentially enabling one to disarm the other by a first strike, will be regarded as a destabilizing factor, though this argument has often been used to keep the arms race going. The construction of underground silos and the strengthening of intercontinental delivery vehicles, the introduction of nuclear submarine forces with missile-launching capability (forces hitherto considered virtually invulnerable because of their mobility and invisibility), the replacement of liquid fuel by solid fuel, and maintenance of some vulnerable forces like bombers on alerts, are all factors which to some extent can be said to have helped to stabilize deterrence. It is generally believed that the more invulnerable the forces, the less temptation for a State to risk a first strike because it would in any event be the target of intolerable reprisals. Improvements in the accuracy of missiles, however, call into question the invulnerability of stationary strategic weapons, since their protection cannot withstand the effects of a very close nuclear explosion. The emergence of precision weapons to be used against hard targets has thus raised the possibility of a counterforce strategy and has given impetus to new doctrinal developments.

If ICBMs in their silos cannot be made invulnerable by virtue of hardening, defence or sheer numbers against a threat of destruction and if the ICBM force is deemed vital by a nation as part of its strategic offensive force, it seems possible that the United States and the USSR could place their ICBM forces in a launch-on-attack status. This would, however, not be a very stable situation. The disadvantages of a launch-under-attack system lie in the possibility of accidental, mistaken launch, and in the new vulnerabilities which such a system might bring. Still one of the super-Powers, in the belief that it is to be vanquished in the strategic arms competition, might implement launch-under-attack, as best it can. Even though this might reduce the provocation to initiate a nuclear exchange, the introduction of such a new element of instability in the balance would be a matter of serious concern.

One aspect of the technological development which should not be overlooked is the effect of increasingly sophisticated technology on the clarity of distinctions between various doctrinal concepts. Distinctions between deterrence, war-fighting, conventional, nuclear, strategic, theatre and tactical are all becoming very diffuse through the development of various weapon technologies. The blurring of these distinctions may have deleterious effects on the possibilities of defining a particular nuclear threshold, although the political and psychological aspects of it are probably more important than the technological aspect.

Besides the technological development there are naturally also other forces that influence the formation of various doctrines, such as political and military environment, historical experiences and traditional views, psychological factors and even environmental considerations.

Nuclear doctrines of the nuclear-weapon States

In the following paragraphs a brief description is attempted of the main features of the nuclear doctrines of the nuclear-weapon States. The description of the various doctrines is made from the perspective of the applicability of the doctrines towards other nuclear-weapon States. As for the possible use of nuclear weapons against non-nuclear-weapon States, these doctrines are discussed in some detail in chapter VII of this report. It may be recollected that there has been only one known case where nuclear weapons have been used, and this was against a non-nuclear-weapon State. However, in the case of several crises or armed conflicts nuclear weapons were used as instruments of pressure or threats against non-nuclear-weapon States. It should be noted here that since the emergence of nuclear weapons, no direct military conflict—apart from certain border clashes—has taken place between nuclear-weapon States, but there have been a great number of military conflicts between nuclear-weapon States and non-nuclear-weapon States.

In discussing in the following paragraphs the doctrines of various countries regarding nuclear weapons, it should be noted that they have historically undergone considerable change, and that there has been a fair amount of interaction between the different doctrines, either through the process of negotiation or through changing perceptions of threats to the national security of those countries. Needless to say, a great deal of evolution of and interaction between doctrines may be attributed to development in weapon technologies as well as to varying aspects of the international relationship.

Nuclear doctrines of the United States of America

Although in the immediate period following the Second World War it was recognized in the United States that the atomic bomb might potentially change all military strategy, this bomb was mainly viewed as a somewhat bigger bomb to be used in the same way other bombs had been used at the end of the war. The United

States had a very small stockpile of nuclear weapons and there was no strong drive to increase to any great extent the size of that stockpile. The United States had a virtual monopoly of nuclear weapons, but no particular doctrine had emerged for the use of these weapons.

In the beginning of the 1950s, however, a re-evaluation of American defence policy was begun, under the impact of the changing world situation and the development of the Soviet Union's nuclear capability. In 1954, the United States Secretary of State, John Foster Dulles, expressed what was referred to as "the doctrine of massive retaliation". Under this doctrine, the United States defence was reinforced by the threatened deterrent of massive retaliatory power. The United States, according to Dulles, reserved the option of retaliating instantly, "by means, at times, and at places of our choosing".[32] That declaration was said to be intended primarily to underscore the preventive nature of the nuclear threat. The declaration did not in itself signify a major change in policy but was a clear expression of a re-evaluation initiated earlier. Neither was it clear that the policy should be interpreted as a warning that the United States would automatically bomb the capital of an adversary in the event of an attack on the United States or its allies over the world. On the contrary, the doctrine might well also be interpreted as a form of limited retaliation—that the United States would not necessarily meet military action where it occurred, but might respond, with or without nuclear weapons, with attacks on strategic targets.

The Soviet Union's first thermonuclear test in 1953 and the launching of the first Soviet Sputnik in 1957 ended the American monopoly of thermonuclear weapons and made it clear that the United States would thenceforth be within range of intercontinental missiles. These two advances of Soviet technology—particularly the latter—had a great psychological impact in the United States at the time.

The increased vulnerability of the United States put an end to the idea of the traditional "Fortress America". For the first time in this century there was a serious military threat to the United

States mainland. The introduction of tactical nuclear weapons in the late 1950s and the emergence of the concept of limited warfare were two convergent factors of readjustment at the level of military doctrines.

Thus, important changes in the nuclear doctrines of the United States took place in the beginning of the 1960s and the doctrine of flexible response was announced. The concept of limitation was underlined in the selection of available means, for fear that a generalized war would lead to mutual suicide.

At the level of limited warfare, greater stress was placed on strengthening the conventional forces of the NATO alliance. Earlier the United States had relied on the threat of massive retaliation to protect itself, but that doctrine was considered to have lost much of its credibility in the face of the development and strengthening of the Soviet Union's nuclear panoply. The view was now that the strategic forces of each side would act as a shield behind which its conventional forces could, if need be, carry on a limited war. The conventional forces should be able to act as a "stopping mechanism" or impose a "pause" in the outbreak of hostilities.[33] The strengthening of conventional forces was said to aim at avoiding recourse to strategic nuclear weapons in so far as possible.

The question of tactical nuclear weapons was debated within the NATO alliance. The alleged preventive and deterrent character of such weapons was weighed against the risk of lowering the nuclear threshold. When the doctrine of flexible response was announced, this in practice implied the existence of flexible and effective conventional forces, if necessary supported by tactical nuclear firepower. The doctrine stated that each case of aggression would be dealt with independently. It meant that recourse to nuclear weapons was not automatic, but not unthinkable when conventional forces were on the point of being overwhelmed by the severity of an enemy attack.

At the level of total war, the United States Secretary of Defense, Mr. Robert McNamara, extended his notion of control and restraint by talking about attacking only military targets in case of war. In a speech in 1962 he declared:

> "The United States has come to the conclusion that to the extent fea-
> sible, basic military strategy in a possible general nuclear war should
> be approached in much the same way that more conventional mili-
> tary operations have been regarded in the past. That is to say, princi-
> pal military objectives, in the event of a nuclear war stemming from a
> major attack on the Alliance, should be the destruction of the enemy's
> military forces, not of its civilian population. The very strength and
> nature of the Alliance forces make it possible for us to retain, even in
> the face of a massive surprise attack, sufficient reserve striking power
> to destroy an enemy society if driven to it. In other words, we are giv-
> ing a possible opponent the strongest imaginable incentive to refrain
> from striking our own cities."[34]

In his speech Mr. McNamara also extended the notion of deterrence and bargaining into the period after the inception of a
general nuclear war, thus negating the idea that deterrence could
only work before the war. Furthermore, Mr. McNamara
announced specifically that the United States had removed Soviet
cities from its first priority target list. He declared that the United
States would not strike Soviet cities unless the Soviet Union
attacked American cities first. In spite of this rather clear expression of the counterforce doctrine, experts gave little credence to
this part of Mr. McNamara's statement, because the technically
feasible options of that time offered limited possibilities of
reaching and concentrating on military targets.

Fifteen years later, however, the then United States Secretary
of Defense, Mr. James R. Schlesinger, was emphasizing the
notion of "options", and more particularly the need for the
United States to possess "forces to execute a wide range of
options in response to potential actions by an enemy, including a
capability for precise attacks on both soft and hard targets, while
at the same time minimizing unintended collateral damage".[35]

The intention of giving United States forces "selective
targeting options" applicable to both "hard" and "soft" targets
has often been criticized for making nuclear war possible, imagin-
able or more real. It is said that a balance of terror based on the

mutual vulnerability of civilian populations held as hostages is still the best guarantee of deterrence, and that any move to mitigate the threat of mutual suicide by shielding the population and the production base thus would dilute deterrence by making war acceptable.

According to the present United States Secretary of Defense, Mr. Harold Brown, a strategy based on the concept of assured destruction alone "no longer is wholly credible".[36] Yet, two years earlier, in 1977, Mr. Brown had declared that "any use of nuclear weapons would run the risk of rapid escalation; a full-scale thermonuclear exchange could result only in a catastrophic outcome for both the Soviet Union and the United States".[37] Considering the different functions that even one and the same expression of a doctrine might serve, the two views are not necessarily totally contradictory. Mr. Brown apparently seeks to retain the option of making a selective nuclear response even if he thinks it improbable that these options would be exercised without bringing about an automatic escalation.

Nuclear doctrines of the Soviet Union

Soviet nuclear doctrines are generally not as openly expressed as is the case in the United States. Soviet thinking on the subject to a large extent has to be deduced from very general statements, from military force dispositions and from Soviet military writing. This sets limits for the general understanding of Soviet doctrines, and at the same time creates a greater degree of ambiguity, which consequently could potentially lead to misunderstandings. This ambiguity is regarded by the Soviet Union as a stabilizing factor and has been characterized by others as a destabilizing force in the global military balance.

As was indicated earlier, the concept of military doctrine is normally used in a broader sense in the Soviet Union than in the West. The content of Soviet military doctrine can be divided into two separate, but interconnected groups of questions—political and military.

The political part gives an indication as to the political aims of a

war and its character, the influence of these factors on the formation of the military forces and the military preparedness of the
country. The military part of the doctrine indicates the means for
the conduct of war and guidelines for the formation of military
forces, the technical equipment of the forces and their preparedness. The nuclear doctrines primarily belong to the military part
of the doctrine but also contain elements of the political part.
While Soviet military doctrine in its general political part
describes itself as defensive, the military part, dealing with strategy, operational art and tactics, lays more emphasis on offence.

In the mid-1950s signs of the formation of specific nuclear
doctrines appeared in Soviet statements and writing. Until then
the atom bomb and its implications for modern warfare had been
ignored or played down. Even when thermonuclear weapons were
developed and tested by both the United States and the Soviet
Union, and thus their destructive power and its implications
known to Soviet leaders, the full consequences of a general
nuclear war did not seem to be openly recognized in the Soviet
Union.

In 1960, however, the Chairman of the Soviet Council of
Ministers, Nikita Krushchev, announced that a new branch of the
Soviet military forces had been formed—the strategic missile
forces. At the same time, he announced that the conventional
forces would be reduced or replaced, because nuclear weapons
"had made it possible to raise our country's defensive power to
such a level that we are capable of making further reduction of
our military forces".[38]

Krushchev's announcements were supplemented by a statement by Defence Minister Malinovsky in 1961, when he stated
that one of the most important points of the Soviet military
doctrine was that a world war—if initiated by imperialist
aggressors—"inevitably would take the form of a nuclear missile
war".[39] Those statements indicated that the concepts of deterrence and massive retaliation played an important part in Soviet
thinking at the time.

These and other statements were followed in 1962 by the publication by Marshal V. D. Sokolovsky of a comprehensive work on military strategy. Here, the devastating effect of nuclear weapons was fully recognized, as well as the revolution of military strategy that they had caused. One central thesis was that a war where the super-Powers were involved inevitably would escalate to a general nuclear war: "It should be emphasized that, with the international relations existing under present-day conditions and the present level of development of military equipment, any armed conflict will inevitably escalate into a general nuclear war if the nuclear Powers are drawn into this conflict".[40]

Regarding war against the Soviet Union, Mr. Sokolovsky wrote: "If a war against the USSR or any other socialist country is unleashed by the imperialist bloc, such a war will unavoidably take the nature of a world war with the majority of the countries in the world participating in it".[41] In 1963, however, a new edition of Mr. Sokolovsky's work appeared. While the second edition—as well as subsequently the third—still contained descriptions of future wars that generally stressed their escalatory nature, some changes in the text implied a more flexible approach. In the above quotation, the words "will unavoidably" were replaced by "might". The following addition to the second edition also illustrates an increasing flexibility as to the use of strategic or tactical nuclear weapons, thus indicating possibilities other than simply strategic massive retaliation: "In working out the forms and methods for conducting a future war an entire number of questions should be considered: how will the war be unleashed, what character will it assume, who will be the main enemy, will nuclear weapons be employed at the very start of the war or in the course of the war, which nuclear weapons—strategic or only operational-tactical—where, in what area or in what theatre will the main events unfold, etc."[42]

A widely held view is that Soviet military strategists are generally inclined to recommend an early use of nuclear weapons. This view is probably a result of the detailed and penetrating way in which nuclear war is treated in Soviet military writing. The impression is formed that it is not the threshold between conventional and nuclear weapons which is the most important, but the threshold of war in general.

Around 1970, however, some signs appeared that strategists in the Soviet Union considered the conventional option feasible even in a general war. A Soviet miltary writer, Colonel-General A. S. Zjoltov, stated without any reservation that "it is completely possible that a war can be conducted with only conventional weapons". He said that: first, war without nuclear weapons is possible; second, even if nuclear weapons are used, these weapons cannot solve all military tasks, thus can the territory of the enemy not be occupied; third, the use of nuclear weapons against some targets may prove not operative; fourth, nuclear weapons can under some circumstances be an obstacle for the advancement of a country's own forces; and fifth, many conventional weapons can be used with great effect against the nuclear weapons of an enemy.[43]

Although this particular statement may not express an official policy, it is an indication that Soviet strategy has perhaps more flexibility than often assumed. Also later formulations of Defence Minister Gretchko seem to indicate that the earlier, almost automatic recourse to nuclear weapons that seemed to be advocated has been replaced by a different, more flexible view, conditioned by the lack of knowledge of how a future war might take shape.[44]

There is reason to believe that Soviet military strategists now seem to consider the possibility of a local (limited) war using tactical nuclear weapons, and even the possibility of a general conventional war. But this does not necessarily mean that the option of massive retaliation has been abandoned as a basic feature of Soviet nuclear doctrines.

Nuclear doctrines of China

Like the other nuclear-weapon Powers, China has repeatedly asserted that it is for reasons of defence that it has built up a nuclear arsenal. Unlike other nuclear Powers, however, China has stated on a number of occasions and in various circumstances that it would never be the first to use nuclear weapons.

China has never openly expressed its views concerning conditions for the use of nuclear weapons or expressed any definitive form of given nuclear doctrine. This has by some been taken as an indication of a "calculated ambiguity" designed to maximize uncertainties about Chinese intentions and capabilities.[45]

Characteristic of China's attitude towards nuclear weapons has been a tendency to downgrade the significance of these weapons. This was derived very much from the judgement on the part of the Chinese leadership that thermonuclear war waged upon China because of the land configuration and population distribution would not produce as extensive damage as it would in some other countries. That was the reasoning stated behind such an attitude of downgrading. Even if Mao Zedong's words about the atom bomb as a "paper tiger"[46] are not necessarily representative, some Chinese statements seem to reflect a belief that nuclear weapons are not so powerful and effective as they appear to be. At the same time other Chinese statements reveal that China has been very much aware of the disastrous implications of a thermonuclear war for China and for the world.

China's defence policy has for many years been based on the concept of a "people's war" on the one hand and nuclear deterrence on the other. In the 1960s the people's war concept was the dominating feature. According to Mao Zedong, an attack on China, whether nuclear or conventional, would have to be followed by an invasion of ground forces, and here the supremacy of the people's war concept would be felt. Hostile forces would be lured deep into China's territory, "bogged down in endless battles and drowned in a hostile human sea".[47]

During the last years it would seem that the adherents of the concept that men are more important than weapons have lost ground. Furthermore, there are now indications that efforts are under way to develop more modern general-purpose forces in order to meet more limited military contingencies than the extremes of nuclear deterrence or mass war. There are also recent indications that China is interested in developing tactical nuclear weapons. Development and deployment of such weapons would probably indicate a fundamental change in the underlying concepts of China's defence policy.

Nuclear doctrines of the United Kingdom

The United Kingdom attaches great importance to its special ties with the United States, including those developed during the Second World War, and has since then particularly conceived its defence plans in the context of a special relationship with the United States. Thus, it has concluded several agreements on military nuclear co-operation with the United States.

However, co-operation in development of nuclear submarines, launchers and warheads was made subject to significant political conditions. The United Kingdom's nuclear submarines have, in fact, been assigned to the defence of NATO, and the United Kingdom is now operating in the context of the Atlantic alliance's "international contribution to deterrence". Nevertheless, the agreements allow the United Kingdom's Government to dedicate its relevant forces, currently assigned to NATO, for solely national purposes, if its "vital national interests" are at stake.

It is therefore difficult to assess the extent to which the United Kingdom would operate its nuclear force independently. In theory, if it chose, it could always withdraw its forces from NATO and declare that it was free to make use of its weapons as it saw fit in any conflict involving its vital interests. In practice, however, such a possibility is remote, particularly since co-ordination, planning and the allocation of targets to be destroyed by United Kingdom forces in time of war all take place in peace-time. It is hard to see which political considerations could justify an autonomous use of British nuclear forces, or under what circumstances they could be embroiled in a nuclear conflict which did not involve the Atlantic alliance. Still, the fact remains that the United Kingdom possesses nuclear forces which could, if necessary, be used independently.

These considerations explain why the debate on strategy within the United Kingdom is today generally bound up with Atlantic defence and why the United Kingdom almost never publicly dissociates itself from the main lines of thought stated within NATO.

Nuclear doctrines of France

France holds that nuclear weapons are, in the final analysis, national weapons. The Government's 1972 White Paper on national defence states that: "Unless vital interests are at stake, the threat of recourse to nuclear weapons has absolutely no credibility . . . In any event, the exclusively national and essentially defensive character of deterrence is evident here . . . If they [the United States and the Soviet Union] recognize objectively that deterrence between them will be effective only when their national sanctuaries are directly threatened, it must be concluded that the defence of Western Europe will not automatically benefit from American deterrence".[48]

The main idea of French deterrence—the weak deterring the strong—is that the weak must have the means to inflict upon the strong a punishment proportionate to the value that defeating the weak represents for the strong. In the French view, therefore, the deterrence of a medium nuclear power is credible even if the size of its strategic nuclear forces could not at all be compared to the size of the forces of the super-Powers.

At the doctrinal level, France has never endorsed NATO's strategy of flexible response, nor has it adopted such a strategy for itself. In French eyes the way to avoid war is to rely on deterrence. In this connexion it should be pointed out that the French conventional ground forces have as their prime purpose to test the determination of an aggressor to continue the war into France. If so, the tactical nuclear weapons assigned to the ground forces could be used to warn an aggressor that he is crossing "the threshold of critical aggression", that is, the point where France would consider launching a strategic response.

No one has ever defined this threshold. The motive behind this uncertainty is to strengthen deterrence. But it also raises the question of the relations between France and NATO. It seems reasonable to believe that the threshold of critical aggression could only be reached after a certain period of warfare in central Europe.

The possible introduction of the neutron bomb into the French nuclear arsenal raises the question whether those weapons will be designed for combat or deterrent purposes. It is perhaps too soon to give an opinion on this subject, but it is not unreasonable to assume that these weapons may be intended to introduce, in the long term, greater flexibility in the display of the French nuclear doctrines.

France regards its strategic nuclear weapons as part of its central systems on the same footing as those of the United States and the Soviet Union and it therefore rejects their inclusion in negotiations on so-called gray area weapons. With their force the French retain a separate European decision centre for the use of nuclear weapons.

Doctrines and security

The impact of the doctrines of nuclear deterrence on international security is difficult to separate from the impact of the very existence of the weapons themselves and the technological development of nuclear-weapon systems. Once the weapons exist—and consequently also the possibility that they may be used—the particular role in international security of the doctrines for their use might not become a matter of primary concern when the actual use of these weapons is contemplated. The specific features of the doctrines, however, determining the conditions for the use of nuclear weapons and the way in which they may be used, are important factors when the implications of the nuclear arsenals for international security are defined. While the latter subject is treated in the following chapter, some observations on the impact of the doctrines, as such, may be worth mentioning here.

One obvious question concerns the credibility of the doctrines, not in the sense whether a State has the means and thus the ability to implement a certain doctrine, but in the sense of the relationship between doctrines and reality. Will the doctrines really prove to be reliable instruments in a crisis situation, or will the situation develop independently of the doctrines? It is impossible to answer this with any degree of certainty, but it must be pointed out that wars have hitherto had a tendency to proceed and end in ways not predicted. The risk of a nuclear war getting out of control is obvious, and might even be likely.

Another question is whether it is possible in reality to retain a distinction between different doctrinal scenarios once a conflict is under way; i.e., is it possible to distinguish between a counter-force attack aimed at destroying military targets and a counter-value strike aimed at weakening the industrial capacity of a State? Having launched a counterforce strike, what assurances could a State have that the adversary would not respond by counter-value attack, aimed at cities, since there would be little point in striking at silos already emptied of their missiles? Moreover, can the first-strike State be counted upon to act with restraint? Would it not be tempted to strike with greater force for fear that the adversary might begin a second round of escalation in the means employed?

All these questions raise serious doubts about the possibilities of keeping developments under control and within the limits determined by doctrines. Nevertheless, different doctrines may have different security implications. Deterrence in the form of massive retaliation—on which the concept of deterrence ultimately rests—has vast consequences for the whole international community in case of failure. While it is difficult to state whether, and to what extent, it has contributed to avoiding war between the super-Powers, it is clear that it has not sheltered the non-nuclear States from the threat of others, nor prevented a number of conflicts involving both nuclear and non-nuclear Powers.

VI

Security Implications of the Continued Quantitative Increase and Qualitative Improvement of Nuclear-Weapon Systems

THE CONCEPT OF SECURITY among nations is very complex and open to different interpretations. In a regional context, States sometimes achieve what is perceived as a higher level of security by entering into an alliance. The same level of national security may be obtained by regional co-operation and disarmament or arms control agreements. It is then recognized that a widened economic and cultural co-operation between States can help foster an increased interdependence. International security can, in this perspective, be seen as the highest "regional" level. In the following paragraphs, the impact of the further spread and development of nuclear weapons on all three levels will be analysed.

Another dimension of security is the somewhat theoretical distinction between reality and perception. Hence, in the military field, capability is distinguished from the intentions for use. The way in which a State assesses its national security will, by definition, depend on its perception of the actual or potential threats to which its security and other needs are subjected and on its capacity to meet such threats. Perception may be critical, especially when it leads a State to conclude that its security is threatened. Even when such a belief is mistaken, it may have a self-fulfilling character, and so stimulate an arms race or an open conflict between States. The national security of a State may be threatened not only by military force but also by political and economic measures. Vulnerability which derives from a dependence on other countries may, however, be turned into a state of mutual interdependence. In this case, hostile action by one country could hurt all and thus be counterproductive.

Only a handful of States so far possess nuclear weapons.[49] The reasons for acquiring them are many: enhancement of national security, the enhancement of national status and prestige, the protection of national independence and freedom of action, the promotion of scientific and technological development, pressures from special interest groups within Governments, and the desire to have a paramount instrument of policy. It is therefore likely that these same motives, or some of them, could be invoked also by other States going nuclear.

It should be kept in mind that the large majority of States are in no position to develop nuclear weapons. A great number of States have renounced the acquisition of nuclear weapons, directly or indirectly, including through adherence to the Treaty on the Non-Proliferation of Nuclear Weapons, the Treaty for the Prohibition of Nuclear Weapons in Latin America (Treaty of Tlatelolco) and other international agreements. At the same time, there are some States, belonging to alliance systems, which rely on nuclear weapons for their security and which have nuclear weapons on their soil and train their troops in the deployment and use of such weapons. With time, the technical and economic obstacles to nuclear-weapon production are decreasing. It will thus require a political will by the non-nuclear-weapon States to continue to abstain from these weapons. At the same time, possession of nuclear weapons by a few States which are militarily significant gives currency to the notion that States which aspire to great-Power status need to acquire nuclear weapons.

Preoccupation among the nuclear-weapon States about vertical escalation of their arsenal has led to a situation in which their capabilities of contributing to regional security have diminished. It is often argued in various international forums that nuclear weapons are today less credible even for limited security pur-

poses. There are those who observe that this situation is not totally unrelated to the world-wide concern over horizontal nuclear
proliferation.

Nuclear weapons and national security

The ways in which Governments define national security
differ. The same can be said about the relationship between
national security and the role of nuclear weapons. The following
sections will consider the super-Powers, other nuclear-weapon
States, and non-nuclear-weapon States, including those with
significant industrial and technological infrastructures.

The super-Powers

The two super-Powers, the Soviet Union and the United States,
maintain the two largest nuclear-weapon arsenals in the world.
They also possess very large conventional armed forces and are
strong economic Powers with a large population, large industrialized capacity, advanced scientific and technological capability
and significant natural resources. From the point of view of
their national security, however, each considers the main threat to
arise from the strategic nuclear-weapon systems of the other
super-Power. It has been shown in previous chapters how these
arsenals have been enlarged and how different strategic doctrines
have been adopted at different times by each super-Power to provide what was thought to be necessary to enhance and protect its
national security. One concern has been the possibility that one of
the super-Powers would attain "nuclear superiority", notably in
terms of a first-strike capability that could be used to eliminate
the strategic weapons of the other. A second consideration per-
tains to the instability of the mutual deterrence situation, how
political, technical or human mistakes could unleash a strategic
exchange with vast consequences.

If one super-Power were to achieve "nuclear superiority" in
some meaningful and lasting sense (if that is possible), there
would, in effect, be only one nuclear super-Power, with the
consequences that this might have for international relations. It is

therefore not surprising that neither seems confident that the other has eschewed the goal of superiority. Even when the two agree to avoid unequal capabilities, each considers that its national security depends on the continual improvement of its forces in order to match, or keep ahead of, comparable improvements in the other's forces. At the same time, it would seem virtually impossible to attain nuclear superiority when the strategic forces are as numerous, dispersed and protected as at present. The argument is more forceful in the opposite direction: because of the vast numbers of strategic nuclear weapons in existence, it should be possible to undertake a major arms reduction without jeopardizing the national security of the two super-Powers.

The same conclusion follows from a consideration of the stability of the nuclear deterrence situation: the more numerous the weapons, the more complex the systems and sophisticated the doctrines, the more likely it may be that the weapons may be used by mistake, be it a political, military, technical or human mistake. There is no foolproof system for the control of nuclear weapons. Various methods may be used to decrease the risk of a mistake, but in spite of all efforts accidents have occurred involving nuclear weapons and they will continue to occur. This is a concrete threat to the national security of both super-Powers. Each is dependent on the "nuclear stability" of the other. One example of this is the false alarm in the United States, on 9 November 1979, of a Soviet missile attack. The attack warning gave the United States military command barely five minutes to react before the first Soviet missiles—supposedly launched from a submarine—were to hit their targets. Yet it was not until a minute after these warheads were to have struck that it was clear that the alert had been caused by a computer error. A war game tape had somehow gone out as the real thing. Other false alarms, such as 3 and 6 June 1980, have been reported.

One further and most important aspect of the stability of the system of mutual deterrence lies with the quality of the continuing nuclear arms race. There are several views as to the roots and causes of the arms race and each may highlight a particular aspect of the problem. In all these theories one must ask, however, what assurances do they provide that the underlying process of research and development will not yield military applications of a destabilizing nature? To put one's confidence in "living with the nuclear arms race" may thus be an ominous investment for the future.

The nuclear arms race has been a major feature of international relations since the Second World War. Sometimes it has seemed as if one super-Power has sought an offensive capability superior to that of the other super-Power. In other cases the mutual mistrust has led both States to seek simultaneously a military capability that each hoped might deter the other party from launching a military attack or convince it that it could not succeed in an attack or would be defeated in a military conflict. The conventional view is then that the military capabilities of the two States are perceived to increase by a process of action-reaction, the end result being *status quo* but on a higher level of armaments. This is often referred to as the arms-race spiral.

This phenomenon could occur even when the two sides were agreed on the principle of parity in their respective forces. The capability of the opponent's military forces has in practice often been overestimated to allow for errors or uncertainty in the available information. The forces judged necessary to match that capability could then also be overestimated by a comparable margin to provide for a reserve capacity. Unless this phenomenon is checked, therefore, the principle of parity in forces could still cause an arms race.

According to another view, the development of new strategic weapons systems is not an action-reaction process but the result of two parallel, but separate, processes driven by independent stimuli in the two super-Powers concerned. Decisions to acquire nuclear-weapon systems (and other capabilities) could be taken in order to satisfy demands of various sectional interests within Governments (interservice rivalry in the military establishment or between other interest groups may be cases in point).

Profound developments of the strategic nuclear systems have

been made possible by very large investments in applied research and military technology. This has provided fuel for the nuclear arms race in that programmes have been funded by one Power just to ensure that the other might not gain an edge in the development of a certain technology. Once this technology has been developed, however, the temptation to take advantage of it is usually difficult to resist.

No attempt will be made to weigh the above-mentioned factors comparatively as elements of the nuclear arms race between the super-Powers. Whatever the character of the nuclear arms race, each super-Power perceives that its national security depends heavily on nuclear-weapon systems and on a continuous upgrading of the capability of those systems. No doubt, the risk of a nuclear conflagration has deterred the super-Powers from allowing any confrontation between them to escalate to global war. It is a lamentable state of affairs, however, that if a full-scale conflict were to occur, the price to be paid would be certain destruction of their own societies and very extensive consequences for the rest of the world.

It was an encouraging development when the two super-Powers agreed to begin their Strategic Arms Limitation Talks (SALT). A detailed discussion of their mutual interest in an improved national security could have had important consequences to the best interests also of the rest of the world. This could have been the case, not only in terms of arms limitations but also for a strengthening of détente and international relations in general. So far, however, SALT has not led to steps of disarmament and has had only limited effects from the arms control point of view. It has rather served to strengthen the super-Power conviction that deterrence must be based on a balance of terror. Against the background of the current impasse in the SALT process, decisions are being taken to increase the size and capacity of the nuclear forces of the super-Powers which are likely in the long term to have adverse rather than positive effects on the level of national security felt in each State.

The other nuclear-weapon States.

The nuclear forces of China, France and the United Kingdom are much smaller than those of the two super-Powers. Still, these arsenals are far from insignificant and include both fission and fusion weapons that could cause vast damage, particularly if used against urban targets.

The States which acquired a medium-level nuclear capability did not necessarily do so solely for the purpose of meeting their requirements of national security as they were perceived. A concern for national prestige may also have been relevant. In the case of France there was the added desire to secure at the same time a capability which might provide a measure of independence from the United States deterrent. Like the United Kingdom, France also sought to exert a certain influence on the use of that deterrent. Nevertheless, once nuclear weapons were acquired, their possession and the ensuing implications have come to have a principal bearing on the national security of the medium-level nuclear-weapon Powers.

It is evident from the large difference in the number of nuclear weapons available to the two sides that the possibility of deterring a nuclear attack by a super-Power depends on the medium-level Power being credibly able to inflict significant retaliatory damage on civilian targets. With a vulnerable nuclear force, a counter-value strategy would need to rely on a first strike against the super-Power. With its nuclear weapons in an SLBM-system, on the other hand, the concern of a medium-level nuclear-weapon State would be the long-term protection and the survivability of that system. Anti-submarine warfare is an area of intense research and development by the super-Powers. From the viewpoint of national security, the isolated deterrence capability of the medium-level nuclear-weapon States thus rests on even more uncertain foundations than those of the super-Powers.

There is finally the consideration that a decision by a medium-level nuclear Power to target nuclear weapons against a super-Power would invite countertargeting by that super-Power. Once having resorted to the use of nuclear weapons, a medium-level nuclear Power would therefore be subjected to a much greater amount of destruction than it was itself able to inflict. This again raises basic questions of credibility for the medium-level nuclear Power.

The non-nuclear-weapon States

Among the various concerns that might prompt a non-nuclear-weapon State to consider acquiring nuclear weapons, the question of the impact on its national security must play a central role. If there are no good security arguments for an acquisition and if, on the contrary, good arguments point the other way, then the case for becoming a nuclear-weapon State should be a dubious one. There is, however, an obvious difficulty in proving this point at a time when the nuclear-weapon States are continuing the development of their nuclear arsenals at a fast pace. Their example is a bad one. It allows a justification for other States to acquire nuclear weapons. At the same time, the technical and economic difficulties in going nuclear are gradually decreasing with time, as discussed in chapter II.

Nuclear weapons have already been used in war against a non-nuclear-weapon State, Japan. It is therefore not inconceivable that a State which found itself in conflict with a nuclear-weapon State might incur the use or the threat of use of nuclear weapons. Such a course of action is becoming increasingly unlikely, partly because of the development of the perception of a threshold against the use of nuclear weapons in war and because of the concern that the use of such weapons would risk a spread or an escalation of the conflict.

This situation may, however, not be a stable one. The super-Powers, in particular, have developed substantial arsenals of tactical nuclear weapons. Their military planners do not exclude the integration of these weapons into the order of battle in certain theatres, particularly Europe. This could therefore lend credibility to the possible use of nuclear weapons in a conflict, e.g., one which began with an attack by conventional forces. The mere existence of nuclear weapons can be perceived as a threat in certain crisis situations. When the weapons exist there is also the possibility of their accidental or unintentional use, leading to wider consequences.

Because of the existence of nuclear weapons, those States which do not possess them have chosen various means to shield themselves against the possibility of nuclear attack. One aspect is the consideration that possession of nuclear weapons might invite a nuclear threat or attack. But some non-nuclear-weapon States consider that the absence of a pledge on the part of the nuclear-weapon Powers that they will not use nuclear weapons against non-nuclear-weapon States under any circumstances undermines the validity of this proposition.

Some States have sought further protection against nuclear attack by entering into an alliance with a nuclear-weapon State, providing a "nuclear umbrella", sometimes by accepting nuclear weapons based on their soil. This question is further discussed in the following section, "Nuclear weapons and regional security". Other non-nuclear-weapon States pursue the obverse approach and seek guarantees that they will not be subject to use, or threat of use, of nuclear weapons by nuclear-weapon States. A number of States have proposed in international forums that nuclear-weapon States should accept treaty obligations to eschew the use of nuclear weapons. Such proposals have generally not been supported by the nuclear-weapon States. These "negative" security assurances are discussed further in chapter VII.

The question then remains to what extent non-nuclear-weapon States could deter nuclear attack by themselves going nuclear and what effect such a move would have on their national security. A significant number of non-nuclear-weapon States have adequate industrial and technological infrastructures to develop fission weapons. A few would also have the technological capability, with time, to construct a nuclear force comparable to that of medium-level nuclear Powers. There are therefore two principal levels of capability to be considered—the capability to deter attack (nuclear or conventional) by a nuclear-weapon State and the capability to deter military threats posed by the conventional military forces of a non-nuclear-weapon State.

Any State which wished to acquire a capability to deter a nuclear attack by a nuclear-weapon State would need to acquire a system which was capable of inflicting significant damage on the nuclear-weapon State and which was not vulnerable to pre-emptive attack. This capability would correspond to that of a medium-level nuclear-weapon State, as discussed above. A major part of the cost of such a system would result from the effort to ensure its survival of an attack and its effectiveness against the defences deployed by a nuclear-weapon State. This cost could be of sufficient magnitude to dissuade even wealthy States from the nuclear option.

Japan is sometimes cited as an example of a State for which acquisition of a medium-level nuclear capability might have been technically and economically feasible. In addition to the very strong public sentiment against nuclear weapons both on moral and psychological grounds, due very much to the national experiences of 1945, there are other considerations regarding security implications of such weapons. During the national debate which preceded Japan's ratification of the Treaty on the Non-Proliferation of Nuclear Weapons in 1976, it was apparent that consensus existed on a number of reasons why Japan's national security would not be enhanced if it acquired nuclear weapons. Because of its high population, Japan is very vulnerable to a nuclear attack. The nuclear deterrent would therefore need to be of a medium-level capability, i.e., well protected and including a sophisticated communications and support system. The cost would have been extremely high. The development of such a force would further-more have required a long lead-time. Finally, there was the pros-pect that, by the time of completion, the arsenal might already be in need of sophisticated systems, including, for example, improved systems and command and control arrangements.

A lower level of nuclear capability which a non-nuclear-weapon State might consider acquiring is to deter a conventional military attack by a nuclear-weapon State. The acquisition of such a "tactical nuclear capability" was given detailed considera-tion by Sweden in the late 1950s and early 1960s. In summary, the discussion led to the conclusion that Sweden's national security would have been weakened rather than enhanced. First, the acquisition of the nuclear force would for reasons of cost have weakened the existing conventional military capability. Secondly, the use of battlefield nuclear weapons, or the threat of their use, would in many instances have invited nuclear retaliation by a nuclear-weapon State. This would have led to a far greater level of destruction on Swedish territory than in the case of a conventional military conflict. Its deterrence strategy would therefore have serious credibility difficulties.

A still lower level of deterrent force which a non-nuclear-weapon State may consider acquiring is a rudimentary to modest nuclear force against a possible military attack by a non-nuclear-weapon State. Such a nuclear force would basically require acquisition of a sufficient number of nuclear weapons to threaten vast destruction and casualties on the territory of an adversary. The difficulty with this scenario is, of course, that the non-nuclear-weapon State to be deterred may also be tempted to go nuclear and it is by no means self-evident that a nuclear confrontation situation would be better than a conventional one for the national security of either State. Rather, there seem to be strong arguments to the contrary.

First, the acquisition of a modest nuclear-weapon force by one State would have a dramatic effect on the local strategic environment. Not only its main adversary but also many other States in the region could be expected to review their level of national security. Those which felt that their national security was in some way affected might decide to acquire a comparable nuclear capability. There is thus the tangible risk that, with time, the whole region would go nuclear. In this context it should be remembered that nuclear-weapon proliferation is a process which is difficult to reverse. Once the knowledge of nuclear-weapon design is acquired, the capability would be easier to re-establish.

Secondly, a basic difficulty with the proliferation scenario is that the new nuclear capabilities established would be rudimentary and modest not only in terms of numbers of weapons but also with regard to the systems for command and control and the methods for protecting the nuclear weapons against attack. This, in turn, may lead to a "delicate balance of terror", thus increasing fears of attack in politically tense situations.

The major result, as in the case of the super-Power nuclear arms race, would be simply to raise the level of destruction that would occur if there was a conflict. With proliferation, the international system of States would move towards a situation where national security would be upheld, not by the best principles of international law, but by the harshest possible rules of punishment.

There is further the general problem of escalation of conflicts to be considered, escalation up to the nuclear level as well as to affect a widening circle of States, including the present nuclear-weapon States. This raises the possibility, e.g., that one or more of the nuclear-weapon States may target some of their own nuclear weapons on an emerging nuclear-weapon State in order to prevent its engaging in nuclear blackmail or threats against other countries.

Because of the many uncertainties and destabilizing elements present in the proliferation scenario it is not surprising that the international community pays close attention to the problem. A State going nuclear could therefore expose itself to a wide range of political condemnation, including sanctions. This may bear directly on national security in the military sense or on various areas of international relations, such as trade, economics and technical co-operation. It shows that commitments not to acquire nuclear weapons have become interwoven into the full complex of relations among States.

It used to be that the holding of a nuclear-weapon test was the demonstration of a State becoming a nuclear-weapon Power. There is today, however, the emerging phenomenon of the "undeclared" nuclear-weapon State. There have been persistent reports that a few States may already have carried out a considerable amount of work towards developing a nuclear-weapon capacity. A State in this category could thus be suspected of having a nuclear capability without actually having demonstrated it, and consequently be regarded as posing a threat of nuclear attack. If so, many of the adverse consequences for national security would be present in the sense that has been discussed above. In this field there are persistent rumors that Israel and South Africa have acquired or are on the way to acquiring a nuclear weapon. Two United Nations studies are presently under way on this subject. There is no doubt that these two cases are a source of concern within the international community.

Nuclear weapons and regional security

There exist various concepts of regional security. Some countries seek their security within the framework of a military alliance, others through agreements on regional co-operation. The regional framework proves as favourable for the enhancement of security through measures aiming at eliminating the nuclear risk, the most striking example of this being the Treaty of Tlatelolco for the creation of a nuclear-weapon-free zone in Latin America.

In an alliance, the nuclear weapons of the super-Powers are intended to play an important role by offering an "umbrella"—either explicit or implicit—to allied countries. In general, the nuclear weapons are then seen as providing a deterrent against all forms of military attack—conventional as well as nuclear.

Notwithstanding the general opposition to the concept of the spheres of influence, particularly as expressed by the countries of the third world, there is a danger that local or regional conflicts may be internationalized through the intervention of the nuclear Powers, with the consequent dangers of escalation.

In Europe, where the interests of the super-Powers are directly engaged, the existence of nuclear umbrellas protecting allied States is intended to reinforce a deterrence situation whereby the security of the region is regarded as indivisible from the security of the super-Powers themselves. Accordingly, any attack by one super-Power on the allies of the other could be regarded and treated as an attack on the second super-Power and might well provoke an initial response, at least with theatre or tactical nuclear weapons, if not with strategic weapons. The deterrent effect would therefore be strong.

Doubts have, however, been expressed concerning the ultimate credibility of the commitment of the super-Powers' strategic forces to deter an attack in Europe, i.e., the willingness of the super-Powers to risk the devastation of their homelands for the defence of their allies. The possibility is raised that an attack might be launched and defended against by the use of theatre nuclear forces on both sides, thus leaving central Europe a nuclear wasteland. This possibility is sometimes referred to as decoupling.

One further consideration which, on the other hand, may re-emphasize the intended function of the nuclear umbrellas in Europe is that the super-Powers possess a regional "strategic" dimension in the deployment of their nuclear forces in Europe. In the context of the alliances, weapon systems such as Pershing II, cruise missiles, SS-20 and the Backfire bomber would have a strategic rather than a battlefield function. There is now, therefore, the prospect that the phenomenon of the strategic nuclear arms race between the super-Powers, and all the questions which it poses for global security, will occur on a smaller scale in the European theatre and pose similar questions on a more limited basis. Such is the somewhat uneasy balance that nuclear weapons provide for the security of Europe.

Also in other regions, where the security interests of the super-Powers may be of a lower order or less directly engaged than in Europe, their nuclear weapons may be intended for, or regarded as providing, an over-all deterrent to attack by one super-Power on an ally of the other. Even without a formal alliance, there could be a deterrent effect by one super-Power's nuclear capability against the possible involvement of the other in a situation of regional conflict in which both sides perceived important national interests to be at stake. The problem here is that the two super-Powers (as do other States) sometimes perceive national interests which go well beyond the promotion of their own national security and affect the independence and sovereignty of other States.

The States of a region can agree on arrangements related to security, arms control or disarmament without establishing the structure of an alliance. Nuclear-weapon-free zones, demilitarized zones and "zones of peace" are examples in point. In these cases, the nuclear-weapon States may also be called on to give certain undertakings in respect of the use of nuclear weapons, the threat of use or even the presence of these weapons in the area. It has been proposed that this could include assurances by the nuclear-weapon States only to use nuclear weapons in their own defence or that of their allies, as well as guarantees not to use such weapons against non-nuclear-weapon States which had formally renounced the acquisition of nuclear weapons. In practice, such proposals have not been universally accepted. There remain, also, the security assurances given by the nuclear-weapon States, quoted in chapter VII. Many non-nuclear-weapon States are not satisfied with these assurances and have sought more specific guarantees.

The foremost example of a nuclear-weapon-free zone is that established in Latin America by the Treaty of Tlatelolco. By this agreement the States of the region undertake not to possess or acquire in any form whatsoever nuclear weapons and the nuclear-weapon States have agreed to respect the denuclearized status of the region. The establishment of such zones has been considered in the United Nations, also with respect to other areas, notably in Africa, the Middle East, South Asia, several parts of Europe, the Mediterranean, the Indian Ocean and the South Pacific. This could provide assurances against both the use of nuclear weapons by the super-Powers and the emergence of new nuclear-weapon States. Nuclear-weapon-free zones thus offer the prospect of precluding nuclear weapons altogether from the considerations of the security of a region. The zone concept will be further discussed in chapter VII.

An even broader approach to regional security is offered by the concepts of "demilitarized zones" and "zones of peace". The Treaty on the demilitarization of Antarctica is the foremost example in the first case; in the second, some efforts are being directed to creating a zone of peace in the Indian Ocean and the Mediterranean.

Nuclear weapons and international security

In a wide sense, international security should represent an ongoing effort to replace the prevailing use of military force in international relations by reliance on the principles of the United Nations Charter and other instruments of international law.

The dominant feature of international relations in the post-war period has been the development of a bi-polar distribution of military force dominated by the two super-Powers. At the same time there has been the dismantling of colonial empires and the admission of a large number of new States into the United Nations family, which has added a new, third dimension to the conduct of international affairs. A number of consequences and conclusions follow from this situation.

First of all, it is clear that nuclear weapons represent an unprecedented threat to international security. As has been amply demonstrated in chapter IV, these weapons would, if ever used in war, inflict extreme and sudden suffering on the population of the world. It is, therefore, in the most vital interest of all States to deal with this threat.

The international community, through the United Nations, has on many occasions expressed its opinion that the achievement of international security requires the ultimate elimination of all nuclear weapons. Even if the risk of nuclear war were very small, it would be a dangerous gamble with international security to try to live in a world full of nuclear weapons for a longer period of time. As, moreover, there is no guarantee that the risk of war can be avoided, the need for nuclear disarmament is imperative. In this connexion, it is important to recall that the General Assembly, at its tenth special session, called upon all States, in particular the nuclear-weapon States, to consider as soon as possible various proposals designed to secure the avoidance of the use of nuclear weapons, the prevention of nuclear war and related objectives, where possible through international agreements, and thereby ensure that the survival of mankind is not endangered. The particular responsibility of the nuclear-weapon States has also been recognized in article VI of the Treaty on the Non-Proliferation of Nuclear Weapons (General Assembly resolution 2373 (XXII) annex), which states:

"Each of the Parties to the Treaty undertakes to pursue negotiations in good faith on effective measures relating to cessation of the nuclear arms race at an early date and to nuclear disarmament, and on a treaty on general and complete disarmament under strict and effective international control."

If there is no progress towards nuclear disarmament the nuclear arms race will go on. Some States may then claim it justifiable to try to acquire a nuclear capability to deter massive attacks against their civilian populations as well as to defend themselves in a conventional military conflict.

It is considered likely by many that the system of security which is inherent in the strategic relationship between the super-Powers, based as it is on a nuclear "balance of terror", has discouraged them for over three decades from initiating military conflict directly with each other. It is also assumed that it has prevented regional conflicts in which either might be involved to escalate to global nuclear conflict. This has not, however, prevented either super-Power from major involvement in large-scale conventional military conflicts on a subglobal level. It is even suggested that confidence in the efficacy of the mutual strategic deterrence at the global level may have had the effect of diminishing inhibitions about super-Power involvement in certain regional conflicts.

To live in a world with nuclear weapons also means that certain innate elements of the nuclear arms race endanger international peace and security. Periods may come when one or the other, and sometimes both, of the super-Powers become less confident about their state of national security. This could occur when one considers that the other has acquired a competitive edge in strategic nuclear capability. It is almost axiomatic that the level of international security is adversely affected when a super-Power becomes uncertain about its own security. In general, the state of international security would thus come to vary with the ups and downs of the nuclear arms race. And it is a fact that the dynamic of the nuclear arms race has caused an increase in the level of nuclear capability at which the deterrence balance is perceived to be established by the two super-Powers.

The super-Powers' reliance on nuclear weapons for their security confers legitimacy on these weapons as instruments of power. The efforts to encourage States to accept binding multi-lateral commitments to forgo nuclear weapons will therefore be hindered unless the nuclear-weapon States themselves demon-strate a preparedness to take meaningful measures towards the elimination of nuclear weapons. Acquisition of nuclear weapons by additional States is, however, likely to undermine inter-national security.

There is therefore a need for the super-Powers to enhance the over-all level of international security by introducing order and predictability into their strategic relationship, by negotiating reductions in and qualitative restraints on the development of their nuclear-weapon stockpiles, and finally by effecting exten-sive reductions in their stockpiles leading to the ultimate elimina-tion of all nuclear weapons. The possibility of this depends upon the level of mutual trust and the inclination to accommodation that exists between them. Each must be confident in the belief that the other considers that national security and national interest are best achieved through negotiation of arms control and disarma-ment rather than by reliance on military force. When a super-Power resorts to force of arms, the climate of mutual confidence upon which accommodation and the basis for agreement must rest is severely eroded. Any such setback has potentially grave consequences for international security.

Vertical proliferation—impact of the quantitative increase of existing arsenals

It is estimated that the United States has about 10,000 and the Soviet Union has about 7,000 nuclear warheads in strategic nuclear systems. In 1967, comparable estimates of the number of strategic warheads were 4,500 and 1,000, respectively. The total number of warheads deployed by the super-Powers nevertheless can be expected to continue to increase initially under SALT II guidelines, given the proviso that more than one warhead can be deployed on some launchers. However, the SALT II agreement, should it come into effect, also foreshadows limits on the total number of warheads that can be deployed.

In practice, qualitative improvements in the nuclear-weapon systems have tended to have a greater bearing on the strategic capability of the super-Powers than straightforward numerical increases. The number of delivery vehicles deployed by one side will, however, become particularly important if it exceeds the number required to destroy the other side's launching platforms. But usually it is not the increased number of delivery vehicles which by itself provides the enhanced capability. It is this factor coupled with the qualitative improvements in the capability of the system.

It is possible to calculate the numerical limits regarding the number of nuclear weapons needed to assure one side the capability to wreak an unacceptable level of destruction on the other.[50] It has been shown, however, that the limits on the development and deployment of nuclear-weapon systems are not based solely on strategic calculations. There may also be internal pressures, in that quantitative increases in strategic systems may affect public and political perceptions of what are comparable levels of strategic power. Even when the strategic posture of one side is not undermined by quantitative increases in the forces of the other, there could thus be pressures to respond so that the over-all level of strategic power of each side *appears* comparable.

Quantitative increases in strategic systems can thus affect the stability of the mutual balance of deterrence, as one super-Power

Figure XIII. Development of Strategic Forces

Number of Warheads

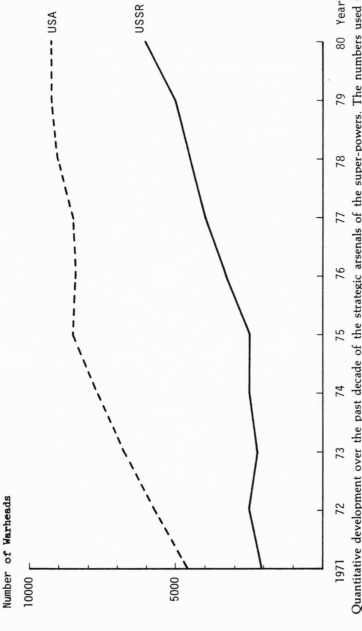

Quantitative development over the past decade of the strategic arsenals of the super-powers. The numbers used to prepare the diagram were the official United States estimates as quoted in the *SIPRI Yearbook 1980.* The actual numbers could be even higher.

may deploy a force capable of destroying the land-based missile launchers of the other. This can in turn be counteracted by an increase in the number of land-based missiles, which have to be targeted. When levels of accuracy are improved, however, to the point where a capability is achieved to destroy one ICBM launcher with one warhead, then it would no longer be efficacious to seek some form of defence by increasing the number of missiles. The increased vulnerability caused by improved accuracy diminishes, to some extent, the strength of deterrence. To counterbalance this situation, a State may have to maintain its retaliation capabilities either through increased invulnerability of its forces or by increasing the number of its fixed land-based missiles.

Quantitative increases of the strategic systems of the super-Powers may likewise prompt the medium-level nuclear Powers to strengthen their nuclear arsenals. When there is an increase in the level of destruction which a super-Power can threaten to inflict on a medium-level nuclear Power in retaliation for an attack, the credibility of the deterrent of that medium-level Power may diminish, unless it also makes the expensive effort to boost the destructive capability of its forces. On the other hand, numerical increases in strategic nuclear weapons are not likely to alter the bearing on the national security of non-nuclear-weapon States which strategic nuclear weapons already have.

Vertical proliferation—impact of the qualitative improvement of nuclear-weapon systems

The super-Powers have, for many years, attained the capability of inflicting unacceptable levels of destruction on each other. The basic strategic concern then has been whether one side might acquire the forces to deny the other this capability. It remains the fundamental question still today.

There are two ways in which the capability to cause unacceptable destruction may be affected (so long as nuclear weapons continue to exist). First, there is the possibility of establishing an effective defensive system, preventing an attacking force from reaching its targets (civilian and military). Secondly, a capacity may be achieved to undertake a pre-emptive strike which would destroy the nuclear force of the other side. These possibilities will be considered in the paragraphs below.

One method of defence would rely on anti-ballistic missiles (ABMs). Under the 1972 Anti-Ballistic Missile Treaty, the United States and the Soviet Union agreed to limit deployment of ABM systems. Since then, the development of technologies upon which an ABM system could be based has not been an area of major endeavour. Nevertheless some research work, for example on laser and charged particle beam weapons, has been carried out which may have applications in ABM technology. A technological breakthrough in one of these fields could thus lead to a reconstruction of the decision not to develop ABM systems.

Methods of passive defence (civil defence), such as shelters and evacuation, could not be effective to the extent of denying unacceptable damage from a major nuclear attack. This is amply evident from the effects of nuclear war described in chapter IV.

Most of the attention is therefore directed towards the trends in the technological development of nuclear-weapon systems which could affect the risk of a pre-emptive nuclear strike. The super-Powers have concentrated in recent years on developing capabilities affecting performance of engines, warheads and guidance systems of missiles. As is apparent from chapter III, significant technological progress has been achieved. Engine developments include more efficient solid-propellant rocket boosters and relatively small and efficient turbofan and turbojet engines. The latter, coupled with development of modern guidance systems, has enabled a substantial technical improvement of cruise missiles. The principal development in warheads has been to increase the diversity and range in weapons intended for theatre use so as to improve battlefield effectiveness and enhance flexibility. The level of precision provided by guidance systems has also increased significantly. This development offers the prospect of achieving a very high "single-shot kill capability" with land-based ballistic missiles and greater accuracy with SLBMs.

In addition to developments in the technology directly related to weapons, advances are occurring in other areas, which have important implications for strategic policies. Improvements in the capability of the command, control and communication systems for the strategic nuclear forces include quicker and more accurate observation by satellites, "over the horizon radar" and other means, enabling better warning of attack. There are also better possibilities for acquiring and analysing such data, which may provide more rapid assessment of possibilities and retargeting of missiles during a nuclear exchange.

These various developments will provide the super-Powers with significantly enhanced capabilities. Improvements in the accuracy of ballistic missiles would increase the effectiveness of a possible first-strike against land-based missile forces. Such accuracy might also create the perception that specific targets could be destroyed with a minimum of collateral damage, thus widening the range of circumstances when a nuclear attack could be utilized.

Acquisition of the capabilities discussed above will not, however, make possible pre-emptive strikes against submarine-based missiles or a strategic airforce that maintains a substantive airborne alert. The relative stability of the super-Power nuclear balance thus remains, at least for the time being. The developments referred to will also be of consequence in other areas of nuclear strategy and this will require review and probably revision of strategic doctrines. The more general consequences, particularly as they affect global stability and security, are considered below.

The development of the capability to engage in nuclear war-fighting and to respond to various levels of attack compels a review of the meaning of what a credible deterrent is. The capability to inflict unacceptable levels of damage in any State which threatened nuclear attack has been regarded as the essence of nuclear deterrence. The capability to launch limited strikes suggests a series of circumstances, however, where threats of retaliation against population and industry may not be regarded as an adequate or credible response. A super-Power may thus not consider that it possesses a credible deterrent on all levels unless it has a capacity both for selective and optional targeting as well as for inflicting unacceptable levels of damage.

Another element to be taken into account is the vulnerability to destruction of the communications systems which support the strategic weapons and provide flexibility to adopt various postures. Destruction of these support systems would put into question the concept of controlled nuclear exchange and seriously undermine the counterforce capability of a super-Power.

A super-Power may consider the capacity to make a controlled or limited response to have certain benefits in times of crisis. It could provide the opportunity to give a measured response to a limited or accidental attack without automatic escalation to a full and devastating response. On the other hand, crisis management may become more difficult. If, e.g., each super-Power would acquire the capability to destroy the fixed land-based missile forces of the other side by expending only a portion of its own land-based missiles, deterrence based on second strike might be undermined. Retaliation to an attack on the land-based force would in turn invite a further response inflicting unacceptable levels of damage.

The barrier against nuclear war is strongest when the threshold to be crossed in initiating a nuclear exchange is very well defined. Adoption by the super-Powers of a wider range of strategies providing for controlled response and limited strikes could thus lead to an erosion of the nuclear threshold. The assumption underlying these strategies is that a nuclear exchange can take place without the certainty of escalation. Another important technological development has been the emergence of systems which can perform both strategic and theatre roles (so-called "grey area" systems). One consequence of their deployment could be to blur distinction between theatre and strategic use of nuclear weapons.

The concept of the long-range cruise missile holds the potential of a radical qualitative development in nuclear platforms for strategic and theatre use. When deployed from long-range bomber aircraft, they would tend primarily to enhance the nuclear strike capability of the bomber, because the survivability of the nuclear warheads would be increased when delivered by these means. Deployment of these missiles from mobile land launchers and all forms of sea-based platforms would also add significantly to the flexibility of the super-Power arsenals. In an indirect way, the development of dual-purpose platforms may also contribute to nuclear proliferation as they might provide a non-nuclear-weapon State with direct access to a potentially highly survivable mode for a nuclear-weapon system.

Deployment of cruise missiles also raises the possibility of the more direct involvement in nuclear conflict of third parties, including non-nuclear-weapon States. An essential quality of the cruise missile is its ability to follow the terrain closely at subsonic speeds at low altitudes. These characteristics suggest that the missile is more likely than other modes of delivery of strategic forces to traverse the air space of States which may lie across its flight-path. States in this category, if they were non-combatants, would be faced with the prospect of de facto involvement in the nuclear conflict. To protest or take action against any transgression of air space may risk conflict with the State launching the missiles. Not to do so may risk conflict with the State to which the missile is directed.

Technical development could also lead to further development of very low-yield nuclear weapons and other types of tactical nuclear weapons in a wider range of capacities. With greater deployment of tactical nuclear weapons and a wider range of tasks assigned, there could be a higher risk of early resort to nuclear weapons in a conflict, meaning that the "firebreak" between nuclear and conventional conflict is narrowed in regions where tactical nuclear weapons are deployed. It is difficult to exclude the possibility that escalation from theatre to strategic nuclear conflict might occur once tactical nuclear weapons were used.

Making an over-all judgement of the full implications of all the qualitative improvements is difficult since the various develop-

ments appear capable of both contributing to and weakening stability. In the most general sense, qualitative improvements may
increase the reliance of the super-Powers on nuclear weapons.
The adverse consequence for international security which nuclear
weapons *per se* are adjudged to have is therefore enhanced.

The acquisition of a capability to engage in nuclear war-fighting may become easier as a result of ongoing improvements of
nuclear-weapon systems. This capability can be expected to make
the strategic relationship between the super-Powers more complicated. Strategic deterrence may, as a result, become more complex and crisis management and control of escalation could be
more difficult. If so, the result could be a higher instability in the
relationship between the super-Powers. If, in consequence, the
super-Powers were to undertake planning for limited nuclear
exchanges, the range of circumstances in which the use of nuclear
weapons was contemplated would increase. If this aspect were to
be coupled with an increasing deployment of battlefield nuclear
weapons, the effect might be that the nuclear threshold would be
lowered.

Horizontal proliferation—impact of the spread of nuclear weapons

When France and China became nuclear Powers it was widely
assumed that this process of horizontal proliferation of nuclear
weapons was gathering an inexorable momentum. It was said that
the process would only conclude when the "Nth" country
acquired nuclear weapons. However, since 1964 no other State
has emerged as a nuclear-weapon State. In 1974, India detonated
a nuclear device, demonstrating a capability to develop nuclear
weapons, but at the same time declaring that it would not build
them. Reports in recent years that other States have worked
secretly to acquire nuclear weapons are a cause for concern, but
developments have not so far borne out the early fears of a very
rapid horizontal nuclear proliferation.

The main reason is that a State will not develop nuclear weapons simply because it has the capability to do so. Such a fun-

damental decision will be based on other factors, as has been discussed earlier in this chapter. Nevertheless, general technological development as well as the increasing reliance internationally
on nuclear power for generation of electricity is leading to a rise in
the number of countries which potentially would have the capability to develop nuclear weapons. This does not mean that operation of a commercial nuclear power reactor automatically gives a
State the capability to construct a nuclear weapon. The recent
International Nuclear Fuel Cycle Evaluation (INFCE) study concludes that fuel cycle facilities are not the most efficient route to
acquire materials for the manufacture of nuclear weapons. However, a State with a small nuclear industry including an active but
not necessarily large research component will have a reserve of
knowledge which, if so applied, could be utilized in a programme
to develop nuclear weapons.

The spread of nuclear power has also been accompanied by the
gradual spread of the sensitive technologies through which fissionable material usable in weapons is obtained—uranium enrichment and reprocessing. With time, the ability to make
weapon-grade material is probably within the reach of some 15 to
25 countries.

In response to international requirements for energy, world
nuclear power capacity rose from about 14,000 MWe to more
than 78,000 MWe between 1970 and 1976. INFCE quotes a figure
of 131,000 MWe at the end of 1979, and a figure of almost
200,000 MWe is estimated for 1985 on the basis of construction
rates today. The number of countries possessing nuclear reactors
will also increase. In 1970, 13 States had at least one nuclear
power reactor with an output greater than 20 MWe. It has been
projected that there will be 27 States in this category by 1981.[51]
World stocks of plutonium present in spent reactor fuel are
expected to increase significantly as a result of expanding nuclear
power programmes, from about 67 tons in 1977 to about 227 tons
in 1985. It has been estimated that the amount of plutonium sepa-
rated from spent fuel will rise from 36 tons in 1977 to 90 tons in
1985.[52] The figures for 1985 are likely to be smaller in view of the

cutdowns in nuclear power generating capacities in comparison to previous plans.

Because of this close connexion between peaceful and military development possibilities, nuclear facilities and international trade in nuclear materials are subject to a wide range of international controls to provide assurance that nuclear industries are not being used for development of nuclear weapons. About 115 States are parties to the Treaty on the Non-Proliferation of Nuclear Weapons. Under its terms, non-nuclear-weapon States parties accept a treaty commitment not to acquire nuclear weapons. They also agree[53] to apply safeguards administered by the International Atomic Energy Agency (IAEA) to all their peaceful nuclear activities in order to ensure that fissionable material is not diverted to nuclear explosive purposes.[54] In Latin America all States except four have committed themselves by becoming parties to the Treaty of Tlatelolco not to introduce nuclear weapons into the region. This Treaty also provides for a special regime of IAEA safeguards. The IAEA also administers a separate system of safeguards whereby States which are not under safeguards of the non-proliferation Treaty can accept safeguards on nuclear material in specific facilities or on particular quantities of nuclear material. Only five non-nuclear-weapon States operate significant nuclear facilities which are not subject to international safeguards.[55] There have been reports of significant amounts of weapons grade material either missing, stolen or otherwise unaccounted for. This is a matter of serious concern, and the view has been expressed that the IAEA safeguards should cover all nuclear facilities.

In recent years, there has been significant debate about non-proliferation and the basis of nuclear trade. States which are major nuclear suppliers have adopted the position that nuclear materials, technology and equipment which could be used for development of nuclear weapons should not be supplied without the recipient State agreeing to apply IAEA safeguards and accept other conditions.[56] Some have adopted stringent national policies designed to seek specific assurances that nuclear co-operation would not lead or contribute to development of a nuclear-weapon capability.

Concern has been expressed that the conditions governing access to nuclear technology, equipment, material and services do not sufficiently recognize the fact that national security and development may depend initially on secure access to energy resources. Some policies of supplier States have been criticized on this score by many States. International consensus exists that all States have the right of access to nuclear energy development and that measures are necessary to prevent effectively the proliferation of nuclear weapons. The current concern in the international discussion of these issues is the search for a practical, agreed basis whereby the requirement of States for fullest access to technology for development is reconciled with the need to insure against the further spread of nuclear weapons.

The success of efforts to develop an international consensus of ways and means, on a universal and non-discriminatory basis, to prevent the proliferation of nuclear weapons depends in large part on the preparedness of the nuclear-weapon States to curb their own nuclear arsenals and achieve disarmament measures. The Programme of Action of the tenth special session, which was adopted by consensus, contains a recommendation that: "In the task of achieving the goals of nuclear disarmament, all the nuclear-weapon States, in particular those among them which possess the most important nuclear arsenals, bear a special responsibility". As pointed out in the paragraph above, the nuclear-weapon States which are parties to the non-proliferation Treaty have accepted an obligation to this effect under article VI of the Treaty. Their fulfilment of this article is one of the central elements of the foundation upon which the Treaty rests. However, there has not been any substantial result in the direction of fulfilment of this obligation.

The technical preconditions for producing nuclear weapons have been discussed in some detail in chapter II. In practice, a State wishing to acquire a rudimentary nuclear-weapon capability would not require a great deal of weapons grade fissionable material. A minimum of 12 warheads might constitute such a force. Although this figure is completely arbitrary, it would provide the capacity to target four cities with three 20 kt. weapons each or 12 cities with one weapon each. Allowing for a risk of failure of one weapon in three, such a force could establish a capability to threaten severe damage to some 3 to 8 cities.

The capability to acquire such a nuclear force is probably within the reach of 20 to 25 non-nuclear-weapon States. The number can be expected to increase as reliance on nuclear power increases, although it is well recognized that development of nuclear power is far from being the optimum path to acquisition of nuclear weapons. In view of the importance of nuclear power for development, States will require the fullest exercise of their right of access to this important resource. At the same time, the international community deserves the greatest degree of assurance available, through appropriate international arrangements, that the spread of nuclear power does not carry with it the prospect of additional States developing nuclear weapons. Reports that States have worked clandestinely to acquire a nuclear-weapon capability are of concern in this context.

VII

Implications of the Treaties, Agreements and Negotiations Related to Nuclear Disarmament

THE DAWN OF THE NUCLEAR AGE brought with it the simultaneous realization of the tremendous potential of nuclear power, and its ominous capability for global annihilation. The destruction of Hiroshima and Nagasaki, both in terms of immediate as well as long-term horror, provided a most tragic practical demonstration of what is, by today's standards, not even considered a minimum nuclear destructive capability. Although the world was nearing the end of its most destructive war, a new pattern of power relationship was already beginning to emerge, and it was perhaps inevitable that military planners would regard the acquisition of nuclear capability as an essential element in the arsenal of a great Power. The nuclear-arms race, therefore, began in the early stages of the Second World War and led before the end of the war to the destruction of Hiroshima and Nagasaki. It is perhaps one of the more ominous paradoxes of history that the horror and tragedy of these two events should have imposed upon military planners the desire, as well as the compulsion, to obtain, in ever increasing numbers and sophistication, the weapons that had demonstrated this horrendous capability for destruction. But whereas the nuclear-arms race began in the early 1940s, the efforts to control this race did not really become manifest until the Soviet Union exploded its first nuclear device and thereby threatened to achieve nuclear parity with the United States.

The very first resolution adopted by the General Assembly in 1946 called for the complete prohibition of nuclear weapons. The initiatives taken in the first few years after the war, including those in the context of the United Nations, sought the comprehensive destruction and elimination of nuclear weapons. Unfortunately, these initiatives did not succeed because of the lack of mutual confidence between the two major power blocs, especially during the period of the cold war. One side did not wish to give up the advantage it enjoyed in nuclear weaponry while the other was determined not to be left behind. Consequently, despite the disarmament talks, the nuclear arms race continued to escalate and led to the development of the hydrogen bomb, intercontinental missiles, orbital satellites, etc.

In the light of the emerging nuclear stand-off between the two sides, some practical and less ambitious objectives were attempted, e.g., to create a nuclear-weapon-free zone in central Europe, but this also failed, and the only redeeming consideration was the fact that in their public positions neither the Soviet Union nor the United States gave up the commitment to the goal of general and complete disarmament.

At the start of the 1960s, the United States and the USSR revived their negotiations towards "general and complete disarmament", including comprehensive nuclear disarmament, and succeeded in reaching agreement on the principles that should guide their negotiations (the so-called McCloy-Zorin agreement of 1961). Divergence of approach and interest appeared almost immediately, however, as became apparent from the two outlines of draft treaties for general and complete disarmament submitted by the United States and the Soviet Union. Efforts by these Powers, and later by some non-aligned and third world States, to bridge the gap between the two positions were unsuccessful. Attention therefore turned to more specific objectives, such as the nuclear-test-ban Treaty, the outer space Treaty, and the non-proliferation Treaty.

The Antarctic Treaty was the first international agreement which, as a Treaty establishing a demilitarized zone, implied provisions that nuclear arms would not be introduced into that zone. It was signed in 1959 by 12 countries (Argentina, Australia, Belgium, Chile, France, Japan, New Zealand, Norway, South Africa, the United Kingdom, the Union of Soviet Socialist Republics and the United States of America) and is currently in force for 19 States.

The Treaty provides that Antarctica shall be used for peaceful purposes only and prohibits, *inter alia*, any measures of a military nature, such as the establishment of military bases and fortifications, the carrying out of military manoeuvres and the testing of any type of weapons.

The Treaty prohibits any nuclear explosions in Antarctica and also the disposal of radioactive waste. However, the norms established in international agreements concerning the use of nuclear energy, including nuclear explosions and the disposal of radioactive waste material, shall apply in Antarctica, provided that all of the original contracting parties and those that show an interest in the continent are also parties to such agreements.

The Treaty created a control system based on national verification through inspection by national observers of the contracting parties which designate them. It also established the right of aerial observation at any time in any area of Antarctica, and the observers have freedom of access at any time to all areas or installations of Antarctica and to all ships and aircraft at points of discharging on the continent.

The provisions of the Treaty apply to the area south of 60° south latitude, and do not prejudice or in any way affect the rights, or the exercise of the rights, of any State under international law with regard to the high seas within that area.

The efforts to prevent the arms race from spreading to outer space were made in the United Nations at the end of the 1950s. In November 1958, the Union of Soviet Socialist Republics submitted a draft resolution in which it proposed, in particular, a ban on the use of outer space for military purposes and an undertaking by States to launch rockets into outer space only under an agreed international programme. In the following years, similar proposals were discussed in the Ten-Nation Committee on Disarmament, the Eighteen-Nation Committee on Disarmament and the United Nations. These efforts sought to establish that States, in the exploration and use of outer space, should be guided by the principle that international law, including the Charter of the United Nations, applied to outer space and celestial bodies and that outer space and celestial bodies were free for exploration and use by all States in conformity with international law and were not subject to national appropriation.

In 1963, Mexico submitted to the Eighteen-Nation Committee on Disarmament the outline of a draft treaty prohibiting the placing in orbit and the stationing in outer space of nuclear weapons or other weapons of mass destruction and also the testing of those weapons in outer space. That same year, the General Assembly adopted a resolution to the same effect.

In 1966 the Soviet Union and the United States reached an agreement on a text entitled "Treaty on Principles Governing the Activities of States in the Exploration and Use of Outer Space, including the Moon and Other Celestial Bodies". The Treaty entered into force on 10 October 1967 and, as at 12 July 1980, is in force for 78 States. The main provisions of the Treaty of interest to this study are as follows:

(a) The undertaking by States parties not to place in orbit around the earth any objects carrying nuclear weapons or any other kinds of weapons of mass destruction, nor to install such weapons on celestial bodies or station them in outer space in any other manner;

(b) The prohibition of all military activities on the moon and other celestial bodies, including the establishment of military bases, installations and fortifications, the testing of any type of weapons and the conduct of military manoeuvres, except for the use of military personnel for scientific research or for any other peaceful purposes, or the use of any equipment necessary for peaceful exploration;

(c) The stipulation that all stations, installations, equipment and space vehicles on the moon and other celestial bodies should be open to representatives of other States parties to the Treaty "on a basis of reciprocity".

Like the Antarctic Treaty, the outer space Treaty is not a measure of disarmament proper, but a preventive one inasmuch as it seeks to avoid the spread of nuclear weapons to areas where they do not previously exist.

Although the Treaty provides for a system of "denuclearization" of outer space, it does not prohibit certain important uses of outer space for military purposes. Thus, the Treaty, in not defining outer space, does not impose any limit on the passage through outer space of ballistic missiles equipped with nuclear warheads from one point on the globe to another. It also proscribes only emplacement in orbit of weapons of mass destruction. The Treaty, therefore, allows the use of the so-called Fractional Orbital Bombardment System (FOBS), i.e., missiles equipped with nuclear warheads which follow a very low orbit—about 100 miles in altitude—and which, before completing a revolution around the earth, diminish their speed, return to the atmosphere and release their nuclear warheads in a ballistic trajectory towards their target. Furthermore, the Treaty permits the use of satellites as a basic element for the control and operation of strategic nuclear weapons and would permit deployment on space-based platforms of ballistic missile defence systems.

The outer space Treaty thus allows a wide margin for the military nuclear use of outer space. This includes the development of the so-called killer-satellite systems which have created a new dimension in the arms race between the United States and the Soviet Union. In the United Nations many countries have expressed their concern at this new aspect of the arms race. As a result the Final Document of the Tenth Special Session of the General Assembly states that, in order to prevent an arms race in outer space, further measures should be taken and appropriate international negotiations held in accordance with the spirit of the outer space Treaty. The subject has also been raised in the Committee on Disarmament in Geneva.

Beginning in 1967, the General Assembly has examined the principle of reserving the sea-bed and the ocean floor exclusively for peaceful purposes. In 1969 the Soviet Union submitted to the Conference of the Eighteen-Nation Committee on Disarmament a draft treaty prohibiting the use of the sea-bed and ocean floor for military purposes, including the emplacement of nuclear weapons in that environment. In 1970 the Committee transmitted to the General Assembly the text of a draft Treaty on the Prohibition of the Emplacement of Nuclear Weapons and Other Weapons of Mass Destruction on the Sea-Bed and the Ocean Floor and in the Subsoil Thereof (resolution 2660 (XXV)). The Treaty entered into force on 18 May 1972 and, as at 12 July 1980, is in force for 67 States.

The parties to the Treaty undertake not to emplant or emplace on the sea-bed and the ocean floor and in the subsoil thereof, beyond 12 nautical miles from its coast, any nuclear weapons or any other types of weapons of mass destruction as well as structures, launching installations or any other facilities specifically designed for storing, testing or using such weapons. Within 12 nautical miles from its coast those undertakings do not apply to the coastal State.

The procedures for verification include the observation of activities in the sea-bed zone and, if it is suspected that there has been a violation, the holding of consultations between the States which have reasonable doubts concerning an activity and the State responsible for it. If the doubts cannot be resolved by means of such consultations, provision is made for the procedure of notifying the other parties so that they may co-operate in the application of further verification procedures, including inspection. If there remains a serious question concerning fulfilment, a State party may refer the matter to the Security Council.

The parties to the Treaty undertake to continue negotiations in good faith concerning further measures in the field of disarmament for the prevention of an arms race on the sea-bed, the ocean floor and the subsoil thereof.

The Treaty does not impose any restrictions on the nuclear military use of the waters superjacent to the sea-bed; submarines equipped with nuclear weapons are treated like any other vessel and are not restricted in any way.

Since the sea-bed Treaty entered into force, a Conference of the States parties was held at Geneva in July 1977 to review the operation of the Treaty with a view to assuring that the purposes of the preamble and the provisions of the Treaty were being realized, taking into account any relevant technological developments. In its Final Declaration the Review Conference confirmed that the obligations assumed under the Treaty had been faithfully observed by the States parties. At the same time, the Conference affirmed the commitment to continue negotiations for the prevention of an arms race in that zone.

Nuclear-weapon testing has played a critical role in the continued development and refinement of nuclear weapons and their delivery systems. This is evidenced by the fact that since 1945 there have been more than 1,200 known nuclear explosions, about 90 per cent of them by the super-Powers. During the 1970s, the Disarmament Decade, a total of 419 nuclear explosions were reported, of which the Soviet Union made 189, the United States 153, France 56, China 15, United Kingdom 5 and India 1.[57] In consequence, there have for many years been negotiations to reach a comprehensive test ban. These efforts have, however, been circumscribed by the desire of the nuclear-weapon States to continue nuclear testing, at least underground.

In 1963 agreement was reached on a partial test-ban Treaty between the United States, the United Kingdom and the USSR. The Treaty gained the general support of the non-nuclear-weapon States but was opposed by two nuclear Powers, France and China, which construed it as being aimed at halting their efforts to achieve qualitative parity in nuclear-weapon development with the two super-Powers. Atmospheric testing by France and China therefore has continued until recently, while the parties to the partial test-ban Treaty have conducted underground tests at an even more rapid pace than before the partial test ban. In 1979 alone, at least 52 nuclear tests were carried out.

An important issue which the partial test-ban Treaty did not address, and which assumed significance especially after the Indian nuclear test in May 1974, was the question of whether or not "peaceful nuclear explosions" should also be prohibited. In the early 1960s, both major nuclear Powers were of the view that such explosions could be useful for economic purposes. Later, United States experts came to the conclusion that peaceful nuclear explosions may have several disadvantages, including economic ones. This position was not shared by the Soviet Union and several non-nuclear-weapon States, although the USSR has indicated that it might be prepared to accept a moratorium on peaceful nuclear explosions under certain circumstances and in the context of a nuclear-test ban. The United States and many other States also concluded that, since that technology could be utilized for nuclear-weapon development, the continuation of peaceful tests would leave open the door to nuclear-weapon proliferation, horizontal and vertical.

The international community has, year after year, called for the early conclusion of a comprehensive test ban. Efforts towards this end have been deployed in the Eighteen-Nation Committee on Disarmament (ENDC), the Conference of the Committee on Disarmament (CCD) and now in the Committee on Disarmament (CD). However, the two super-Powers have maintained a general reluctance to discuss and negotiate on the Treaty in depth in these multilateral forums. The issue of verification has remained one of the main but not the only difficulty in the way of an agreement for a comprehensive test ban. Another difficulty is the alleged value of some continued testing to maintain the reliability of strategic stockpiles. Since 1977, the United States, USSR and the United Kingdom have conducted separate negotiations on a test-ban treaty. The information provided about these negotiations is, however, not substantive. In the absence of a conclusion of the trilateral negotiations, however, the Committee on Disarmament has been unable to conduct detailed negotiations on the subject, despite repeated requests by the General Assembly to do so. The proposal has also been made many times that a moratorium be called for all nuclear testing pending agreement on a comprehensive test ban. A study of the comprehensive test-ban issue has been prepared by the Secretary-General with the assistance of a group of experts and presented to the Committee on Disarmament (CD/86).

In reporting on the state of their negotiations to the Committee on Disarmament, the three nuclear-weapon States concerned have not yet provided details of what elements of a comprehensive test ban may have been agreed upon among them. Successive resolutions of the General Assembly have reflected the view that a test ban should be comprehensive and stop all nuclear tests in all environments for all time. The importance of a comprehensive test ban as a measure to restrain vertical proliferation is the obstacle it would create to qualitative improvement of nuclear-weapon systems by denying opportunities to test new designs for warheads.

Bilateral negotiations between the United States and the USSR resulted in 1975 in an interim agreement to prohibit nuclear testing above an explosion yield of 150 kt. effective 31 March 1976. It was felt by many that this threshold test ban, instead of providing a step towards a comprehensive test ban, had legitimized nuclear testing below the 150 kt. level. This level was, in any case, high enough to permit almost all the nuclear tests which the super-Powers might need to continue improving their nuclear weaponry. Although the agreement did not originally address the question of peaceful nuclear explosions, these were included, a year later, in the ban of tests above the 150 kt. level. The Treaty has not, however, entered into force, but its provisions seem so far to have been observed.

In the late 1950s to early 1960s many countries brought the question of the spread of nuclear weapons to the forefront of world attention. The reason was both the fear that emergence of many new members of the atomic club would multiply the risk for an outbreak of nuclear war and a particular concern related to the use of nuclear weapons in Europe. In 1967, the United States and the USSR submitted separate but identical drafts of a nuclear non-proliferation treaty to the Geneva Conference of the Committee on Disarmament.

The foundation for the nuclear non-proliferation Treaty can be viewed as a bargain struck between three general considerations: first, the commitment by the nuclear-weapon States not to transfer nuclear weapons or the control thereof and the commitment by non-nuclear-weapon States not to acquire nuclear weapons as well as to accept international safeguards on their nuclear industry; second, the undertaking by parties in a position to do so to facilitate to the fullest extent possible development of nuclear energy for peaceful purposes, especially in non-nuclear-weapon States with due regard to the needs of developing areas of the world; and third, the obligations of the nuclear-weapon States under Article VI of the Treaty to undertake in good faith negotiations on disarmament.

In order to meet the concern of non-nuclear-weapon States about their vulnerability to nuclear attack or blackmail, the USSR, the United Kingdom and the United States made statements of policy in the Security Council to come to the assistance, through the Security Council, of a non-nuclear-weapon State, party to the non-proliferation Treaty, subjected to aggression or threat of aggression with nuclear weapons. These declarations were noted in Security Council resolution 255 (1968). Many non-nuclear-weapon States parties to the non-proliferation Treaty, however, expressed their dissatisfaction with these arrangements and stressed the need for effective security assurances.

The non-proliferation Treaty is regarded by many as an important achievement in the area of nuclear-arms regulation. The Treaty entered into force in 1970 and the number of parties has increased to about 115 States. The operation of the non-proliferation Treaty was reviewed in 1975 and a second review conference took place in 1980. Those States which have chosen not to adhere to the Treaty have criticized what they consider to be the inequality in and the discriminating character of the Treaty in explaining their decision to reject it.

In the period since the Treaty entered into force, several developments have altered the international environment in which the non-proliferation Treaty operates and affected the perceptions of the Treaty. There has been a lack of progress in the super-Power negotiations on nuclear disarmament; a number of States are concerned at the possibility of the spread among States of nuclear explosive capability and many States are anxious to obtain access to secure sources of energy, including nuclear energy.

In one development, some supplier countries took steps outside the non-proliferation Treaty structive to place conditions on supply of nuclear material, equipment and technology. These include the guidelines of the Nuclear Suppliers Group (London Club). Some supplier countries maintained that these guidelines were framed out of concern for the need to strengthen non-proliferation arrangements. In the view of many other countries, however, these guidelines have amounted to a reinterpretation of some of the Treaty provisions. Also, some countries expressed dissatisfaction that measures taken by certain supplier States, individually and jointly, place greater restrictions and controls on the peaceful uses of nuclear technology.

These developments have sharpened differences among States over the general questions of non-proliferation and safeguards arrangements and the terms of nuclear trade. A principal issue is how concern by supplier States, individually or jointly, to see tighter non-proliferation control should be reconciled with the desire of other States for greater access to nuclear technology for peaceful purposes and economic development. It is in this perspective that the Final Document of the Tenth Special Session of the General Assembly pointed to the need for development of an "international consensus" on the question of nuclear non-proliferation and the peaceful use of nuclear energy. In respect of the non-proliferation Treaty, many parties have emphasized their view that the efficacy of the Treaty as a measure of nuclear arms control depends upon maintenance of the balance of obligations between the nuclear-weapon States and non-nuclear-weapon States which constitute the foundation upon which the Treaty rests.

One measure of non-proliferation has gained increasing international support in recent years—the establishment of nuclear-weapon-free zones. The early proposals for such zones were made for areas, such as central Europe, where nuclear weapons were already deployed. The only substantive agreement, however, is the Treaty for the Prohibition of Nuclear Weapons in Latin America which for many years was promoted by Mexico and other Latin American States.

This Treaty (often referred to as the Treaty of Tlatelolco, after the name of its place of signature) is the only international instrument agreed upon so far establishing a zone free of nuclear weapons in a populated region. Opened for signature in 1967, the Treaty also established a system of control through a permanent supervisory body: the Agency for the Prohibition of Nuclear Weapons in Latin America (OPANAL).

The main obligations of the parties to the Treaty are to undertake to use exclusively for peaceful purposes the nuclear material and facilities which are under their jurisdiction, and to prohibit and prevent in their respective territories:

(a) The testing, use, manufacture, production or acquisition by any means whatsoever of any nuclear weapons, by the parties themselves, directly or indirectly, on behalf of anyone else or in any other way;

(b) The receipt, storage, installation, deployment and any form of possession of any nuclear weapons, directly or indirectly, by the parties themselves, by anyone on their behalf or in any other way.

The Treaty reaffirms the right of the contracting parties to use nuclear energy for peaceful purposes, in particular for their economic development and social progress. This includes the right to conduct nuclear explosions for peaceful purposes provided that no obligations of the Treaty are violated.

The Treaty is in force for 22 States of the region which have waived the requirements laid down for its final entry into force. Two States, Brazil and Chile, have signed and ratified the agreement but have not waived these requirements so that the Treaty is not in force for them. Brazil has officially declared that it considers itself bound, in accordance with the norms of international law, not to engage in acts which infringe the objectives of the Treaty of Tlatelolco. One State, Argentina, has signed and, during the tenth special session of the General Assembly, announced that it would ratify the Treaty, and two States of the region, Cuba and Guyana, have not yet signed it. Two countries which recently became independent, Saint Lucia and Dominica, have not yet become parties.

The Treaty contains two Additional Protocols which set forth obligations to be undertaken by States outside the region. Additional Protocol I establishes that the statute of nuclear-weapon-free zone also applies to territories situated within the zone of application of the Treaty which *de jure* or *de facto* are under the jurisdiction of States outside the region. This Protocol has been ratified by the Netherlands and the United Kingdom and signed by the United States and France.

Under Additional Protocol II the nuclear-weapon States undertake to fully respect "the status of denuclearization of Latin America", and not to use or threaten to use nuclear weapons against the Parties to the Treaty. All nuclear-weapon States have ratified Additional Protocol II.

As a reaction to the French nuclear testing in the Sahara, several African countries proposed that Africa should be declared a denuclearized zone. The OAU summit in 1963 adopted the "Declaration of the Denuclearization of Africa". The establishment of the African zone has, however, not been realized principally because of the possibility of South Africa's acquiring a nuclear-weapon capability and of the Middle East situation. Relevant General Assembly resolutions have repeatedly called for termination of nuclear co-operation with the racist régime of South Africa. These efforts acquired a special urgency in the light of reports in 1979 that a nuclear explosion may have taken place off the coast of South Africa. In view of these reports, a special United Nations expert group has been appointed to study the possible nuclear-weapon capabilities of South Africa.

The establishment of a nuclear-weapon-free zone in the region of the Middle East was initially proposed in 1974 by Iran, later joined by Egypt. The General Assembly, in supporting this objective, has called on the States in the region to accede to the non-proliferation Treaty or give solemn assurances to the Security Council that they will not acquire or develop nuclear weapons. Israel has refused to accede to these calls and instead posed the pre-conditions of direct negotiations between the States of the region.

After the Indian nuclear test in 1974, Pakistan proposed the creation of a nuclear-weapon-free zone in South Asia. The proposal has, however, been opposed by India, which objected to the General Assembly taking up the question on the grounds that the region was not suitable for a nuclear-weapon-free zone. However, all the States in the region of South Asia have expressed their determination to keep their countries free of nuclear weapons, and the United Nations has asked that no action should be taken by the States of the region which might deviate from this objective. The question of establishing a nuclear-weapon-free zone in South Asia has been dealt with in several resolutions of the Assembly, which is keeping the subject under consideration.

At various times proposals have been made for nuclear-weapon-free zones in other parts of the world, including the South Pacific and different parts of Europe.

The establishment of nuclear-weapon-free zones on the basis of arrangements freely arrived at among the States of the region concerned constitutes an important disarmament measure. There is, however, a need for greater support from the international community to get further progress in solving the many practical and legal problems involved.

The international community attaches the highest priority to the control, reduction and ultimate elimination of all nuclear weapons. This goal has been reaffirmed in the Final Document of the Tenth Special Session of the General Assembly. A comprehensive study on the question of nuclear-weapon-free zones in all of its aspects was undertaken and a report produced under the auspices of CCD in the summer of 1975.

Since 1969, the United States and the USSR have conducted

bilateral Strategic Arms Limitation Talks (SALT). The SALT I agreement was signed in 1972; it put a five-year interim ceiling on the strategic arsenals that formally, if not in reality, expired in 1977; it also limited the anti-ballistic missile systems of the United States and the USSR to two each, a figure that was reduced to one in 1974. While the symbolic aspect of the SALT I agreement remains both significant and considerable, its practical value, in terms of disarmament, was not very substantial, since both Powers had already come to the conclusion that ABM systems were too costly and, ultimately, ineffective. The United States has dismantled even the one ABM system it was allowed under SALT I.

The next stage of the SALT negotiations took nearly seven years before the SALT II treaty was signed in June 1979. It is constructed on the premise of strategic nuclear equivalence between the United States and the USSR. Under the agreement there would be an over-all ceiling on the number of strategic nuclear delivery systems for both parties. These systems are ICBM and SLBM launchers, heavy bombers and long-range air-to-surface ballistic missiles. The initial ceiling on these subsystems would be 2,400, as agreed at the Vladivostok summit in 1974. This limit would be reduced to 2,250 by the end of 1981. Within this over-all limit would exist the following sublimits:

(a) A sublimit of 1,320 on the number of launchers of MIRVed ICBMs and SLBMs, long-range air-to-surface ballistic missiles equipped with MIRV, and bombers equipped for long-range cruise missiles;

(b) A limit of 1,200 launchers of MIRVed ICBMs, SLBMs and ASBMs;

(c) And of this number, no more than 820 launchers of MIRVed ICBMs.

The SALT II treaty does not exclude an expansion of the nuclear arsenals of the super-Powers in certain directions, e.g., the development of the MX missile and the limited deployment of cruise missiles by the United States, and the deployment of the

"Backfire" bomber and improved strategic missiles by the Soviet Union. Such weapon systems already planned, and within treaty limits, will if procured continue to raise spending levels of the super-Powers and their allies. The strategic forces of the two Powers now contain more than 15,000 nuclear bombs and warheads. The SALT II treaty is clearly an arms control agreement. It still remains for the two super-Powers to ratify the agreement.

The Final Document of the Tenth Special Session of the General Assembly, while asking for the conclusion, at the earliest possible date, of the SALT II agreement, stated that that agreement should be followed promptly by further strategic arms limitation negotiations between the United States and the USSR leading to agreed significant reductions of and qualitative limitations on strategic arms which would constitute an important step in the direction of nuclear disarmament and, ultimately, of the establishment of a world free of such weapons. The SALT II agreement, and the debate it has evoked, demonstrates the difficulty of establishing a common understanding of what constitutes an equitable balance of power. The SALT III negotiations will be even more complicated because they may have to take into account the relationship between strategic and theatre nuclear forces of the two sides, besides dealing with the constant qualitative improvements being introduced in their nuclear arsenals.

Besides the agreements mentioned a number of other treaties, mostly on confidence-building measures relevant to nuclear weapons, were also negotiated. Table 6 gives a list of such treaties.

A recommendation for the total prohibition of the use of nuclear weapons was adopted by the General Assembly in 1961 and reaffirmed in 1978. Most of the nuclear Powers have, however, not accepted this proposal.

It has also been suggested that agreement should be reached among the nuclear Powers for the non-first-use of nuclear weapons. Among the nuclear Powers, China has made such a pledge of non-first-use. The Soviet union and its allies in the Warsaw Treaty have proposed a non-first-use agreement to the NATO countries in the context of Europe. The NATO countries, however, feel that they are at a disadvantage in the conventional forces in Europe and, therefore, are not willing to give up the option of the first-use of nuclear weapons as means of self-defence against a superior conventional attack. The Soviet Union has proposed that agreement be reached on the non-first-use of both nuclear and conventional weapons. It has, however, been pointed out that such initiatives can succeed only if they are broadened to evolve a general agreement for the non-first-use of

Table 6: Strategic agreements and treaties

Treaty	Entry into force
United States-USSR Hot-Line Agreement	20 June 1963
United States-USSR Hot-Line Modernization Agreement	30 September 1971
Amended	29 April 1975
United Kingdom-USSR Hot-Line Agreement	27 October 1967
United States-USSR Nuclear Accident Agreement	30 September 1971
United States-USSR Agreement on the Prevention of Incidents on and over the High Seas	25 May 1972
Protocol	22 May 1973
ABM Treaty	3 October 1972
Protocol	25 May 1976
Interim Agreement (SALT I)	3 October 1972 expired on
Protocol	3 October 1977
Standing Consultative Commission	21 December 1972
Protocol	30 May 1973
United States-USSR Agreement on the Prevention of Nuclear War	22 June 1973
Threshold Test-Ban Treaty	—
Peaceful Nuclear Explosions Treaty	—
United States-USSR Vladivostok Accord	24 November 1974
France-USSR Nuclear Accident Agreement	16 July 1976
United Kingdom-USSR Nuclear Accident Agreement	10 October 1977
Limitation of Strategic Offensive Arms (SALT II)	—
Protocol	—

nuclear weapons, and are linked also with a balance between conventional forces.

Many non-nuclear-weapon States have urged the nuclear-weapon States to extend credible and effective assurances not to use or threaten to use nuclear weapons. Such assurances could take the form of "positive" guarantees, i.e., assistance as among allies in the case of nuclear threat or blackmail as well as "negative" assurances that the nuclear-weapon States will not use or threaten to use such weapons against non-nuclear-weapon States. The United States, the USSR and the United Kingdom have stated their inability to go beyond Security Council resolution 255 (1968) in extending "positive" guarantees, although Article 51 of the United Nations Charter could be interpreted as providing for collective defence against aggression with conventional as well as nuclear weapons. On the other hand, general support has been evoked by the idea of "negative" security assurances to non-nuclear-weapon States. But the existing pledges are not unconditional.

In 1976 the General Assembly invited the nuclear-weapon States to extend assurances against the use or threat of use of nuclear weapons to non-nuclear-weapon States "which are not parties to the nuclear security arrangements of the nuclear Powers." At the tenth special session of the General Assembly, the nuclear Powers made unilateral declarations on the question. With one exception, these declarations were conditional in nature and limited in scope. The Final Document, in paragraph 32, urged the nuclear-weapon States to conclude "effective arrangements, as appropriate, to assure non-nuclear-weapon States against the use or the threat of use of nuclear weapons". A year later, Pakistan and the Soviet Union made separate proposals for the consideration of an international convention on this subject. The Committee on Disarmament undertook an in-depth consideration of the subject during its first session in 1979, and noted that there was no objection in principle to the adoption of a draft convention, although the difficulties involved were also pointed out. Negative guarantees if agreed would provide a basis for negotiations on a non-use pledge.

The non-use pledges made by the nuclear Powers during the tenth special session of the General Assembly are:

United States

"The United States will not use nuclear weapons against any non-nuclear State party to the non-proliferation Treaty or to any comparable internationally binding commitment not to acquire nuclear explosive devices, except in the case of an attack on the United States, its territories or armed forces, or its allies, by such a State allied to a nuclear-weapon State or associated with a nuclear-weapon State in carrying out or sustaining the attack." (A/S-10/AC.1/PV.9)

Soviet Union

"The Soviet Union declared that it will never use nuclear weapons against those States which renounce the production and acquisition of nuclear weapons and have no nuclear weapons on their territories. We are ready to conclude special agreements to that effect with any such non-nuclear State. We call upon all other nuclear Powers to follow our example and assure similar obligations." (A/S-10/AC.1/4)

United Kingdom

"I accordingly give the following assurance, on behalf of my Government, to non-nuclear-weapon States which are parties to the non-proliferation Treaty or to other internationally binding commitments not to manufacture or acquire nuclear explosive devices: Britain undertakes not to use nuclear weapons against such States except in the case of an attack on the United Kingdom, its dependent territories, its armed forces or its allies by such a State in association or alliance with a nuclear-weapon State." (A/S-10/PV.26)

France

"In terms of their security, the decision by the States of a region to preserve a nuclear-free status should entail an obligation for the nuclear-weapon States to refrain from seeking a military advantage from this situation. Nuclear-weapon States should in particular preclude, according to a formula to be defined, any use or threat of use of nuclear weapons against States that are part of a nuclear-free zone." (A/S-10/PV.3)

China

"We have . . . on many occasions stated that we will at no time and in no circumstances be the first to use nuclear weapons . . . A measure of urgency is for all nuclear countries to undertake not to resort to the threat or use of nuclear weapons against the non-nuclear countries and nuclear-free zones." (A/S-10/PV.7)

VIII

Conclusion
"The perpetual menace to human society"

THE DAWN OF THE NUCLEAR AGE brought with it the simultaneous realization of the tremendous potential of nuclear power and its ominous capability for global annihilation. The destruction of Hiroshima and Nagasaki, both in terms of immediate as well as long-term horror, provided the most tragic demonstration of what is, by today's standards, not even considered a "minimum nuclear destructive capability". A year before these events, the Danish nuclear physicist and Nobel Laureate Niels Bohr sent identical letters to President Roosevelt and Prime Minister Churchill in which he said, "The fact of immediate preponderance is that a weapon of unparalleled power is being created which will completely change all future conditions of warfare . . . Unless, indeed some agreement about the control of the use of the new active materials can be obtained in due time, any temporary advantage, however great, may be outweighed by a perpetual menace to human society". But these prophetic words went unheeded even as the world was nearing the end of its most destructive war. A new pattern of power relationship was already beginning to emerge, and it was perhaps inevitable that military planners would regard the acquisition of nuclear weapons as an essential element in the arsenal of a great Power. But it is one of the more ominous paradoxes of history that the horror and tragedy of Hiroshima and Nagasaki should have imposed upon military planners the desire, as well as the compulsion, to obtain, in ever increasing numbers and sophistication, the weapons that had demonstrated this horrendous capability for destruction. As a result, nuclear weapons have now become a "perpetual menace to human society", in Bohr's words.

Even if the arms race is not a new phenomenon, mankind's present predicament is certainly unique. Whereas most if not all previous instances of competitive arms build-up and rivalries in weapon development have eventually culminated in conflict on the battlefield, the present situation makes such a dénouement unthinkable. The development of nuclear weapons has, at least for the present, drastically altered all military strategic thinking. Never before have States been in a position to destroy the very basis of the continued existence of other States or regions; never before has the destructive capacity of weapons been so immediate, complete and universal; never before has mankind been faced, as today, with the real danger of self-extinction.

Still, the nuclear arsenals in the world have continued to grow in numbers and in their destructive capability. There exist today at least 40,000 to 50,000 nuclear weapons, the combined explosive power of which is believed to be equivalent to that of more than one million Hiroshima bombs or, to put it differently, some 13 billion tons of TNT, which represents more than 3 tons for every man, woman and child on earth. In spite of this, the number of warheads continues to increase, as does the accuracy with which these weapons can be delivered. As a consequence, the lethality and effectiveness of the arsenals are enhanced much more than a numerical comparison of strategic launchers or warheads would indicate. Large numbers of nuclear weapons can now be used strategically in situations other than a mass attack on the homelands of the super-Powers. There is also a growing capacity for "theatre" use of tactical nuclear weapons which pose a threat to many States, for instance in Europe. Thus, the nuclear-weapon Powers are today prepared for rapid use of their tactical nuclear weapons in a war and for escalation of the level of nuclear violence. Nuclear overkill is everywhere.

The development of nuclear-weapon technology has created an important dimension in the arms race. It is clear that in many cases technology dictates policy instead of serving it and that new weapon systems frequently emerge not because of any military or security requirement but because of the sheer momentum of the technological process. In particular, the successively enhanced accuracy of the strategic delivery systems fuels the arms race by creating a "duelling" situation between these systems. This general trend, that technology rather than policy leads, carries with it an intrinsic danger. Technology by itself is blind to the dangers of the arms race; it leads to wherever the principles of science and engineering may carry. In this situation it is imperative that statesmen and political leaders accept their responsibility. If they do not, the arms race is certain to go out of control.

If this report has proved nothing else, it should at least have served to demonstrate the catastrophic consequences which would result if the nuclear arsenals of today or tomorrow were ever unleashed in war. There are perhaps some who wish to draw comfort from calculations that it may be difficult to kill outright every man, woman and child on earth even in a nuclear war. But such calculations are empty exercises. The danger of the annihilation of human civilization should not be made the subject of theoretical arguments, but be used as a basis for creating a common awareness of the alarming situation the world is facing today and of the need for exercising the political will to search for acceptable solutions.

In a nuclear war, the nuclear-weapon States themselves may suffer the heaviest casualties and the most extensive damage. However, all nations in the world would experience grave physical consequences. Radioactive fallout could be a serious problem especially in countries adjacent to the belligerent States, and during the decades after a major nuclear war, fallout would take a toll of millions world-wide, in present and future generations. Even more serious than radioactive fallout, however, would be the global consequences of a large nuclear war on the world economy and on vital functions of the international community. The sudden collapse of many of the world's leading trading nations as well as of established mechanisms for international transactions would lead to profound disorganization in world affairs and leave most other nations, even if physically intact, in desperate circumstances. Widespread famines could occur, both in poor developing countries and in industrialized nations. Those starving to death might eventually outnumber the direct fatalities in the belligerent countries. Even non-belligerent States might enter a downward spiral leading to utter misery for their populations, and almost all would suffer a loss of standards corresponding to many decades of progress. Economic conditions such as these might trigger latent political instabilities, causing upheavals and civil and local wars.

In the face of the enormity of the destruction that would be caused by a nuclear war, there must be a decisive concern with the stability of the global deterrence situation. The argument of the stability of the balance is one which gives the proponents of deterrence great difficulty. In order to claim that it is possible to continue, forever, to live with nuclear weapons, the balance must be maintained at all times irrespective of any technological challenges that may present themselves as a result of the arms race. In addition, there must be no accidents of a human or technical nature, which is an impossible requirement as shown by the various incidents of false alarms and computer malfunctioning that are reported from time to time. Sooner or later one of these incidents may give rise to a real accident with untold consequences. For these and other reasons it is not possible to offer a blanket guarantee of eternal stability of the deterrence balance and no one should be permitted to issue calming declarations to this effect. The consequences of being wrong are too great. The chances of being wrong are too obvious. This is an important reason why the Final Document of the Tenth Special Session of the General Assembly, adopted by consensus on 30 June 1978, stated categorically, in paragraph 13, that "Enduring international peace and security cannot be built on the accumulation of weaponry by military alliances nor be sustained by a precarious balance of deterrence or doctrines of strategic superiority".

Even if the balance of deterrence was an entirely stable phenomenon, there are strong moral and political arguments against a continued reliance on this balance. It is inadmissible that the prospect of the annihilation of human civilization is used by some States to promote their security. The future of mankind is then made hostage to the perceived security of a few nuclear-weapon States and most notably that of the two super-Powers. It is furthermore not acceptable to establish, for the indefinite future, a world system of nuclear-weapon States and non-nuclear-weapon States. This very system carries within it the seed of nuclear-weapon proliferation. In the long run, therefore, it is a system that contains the origins of its own destruction.

There is the further fact that the doctrines of nuclear deterrence have to a certain extent developed in conjunction with technology and they have thus become increasingly sophisticated as the range of means available for their implementation has become wider, more complex and more diversified. Doctrines, in a sense, are fictions built upon various hypothetical scenarios of nuclear war. Also for this reason, they have grown too complicated and sophisticated. This trend is undermining the credibility of the doctrines even among those who subscribe to the usefulness of nuclear weapons. It is therefore highly questionable whether the doctrines of deterrence would prove to be reliable instruments of control in a crisis. In any case, events do develop independently of the doctrines and no one can say with assurance that reality will unfold itself according to what may have been expected or in line with what was foreseen by virtue of the doctrines.

In spite of all arguments, some countries have chosen to base their security perceptions on nuclear-weapon systems, in the hope that the balance of deterrence may remain stable. In particular, the super-Powers perceive that nuclear weapons support their national security both by deterring a direct conflict between them and by increasing their influence in other areas of the world. At the same time, both are concerned that the other might achieve nuclear superiority. In the absence of verifiable measures of disarmament, these concerns are projected as justifying further quantitative increases and qualitative developments of their nuclear arsenals. But the doubtful stability of deterrence may well decrease as a result of the nuclear arms race, even if both sides have agreed to seek nuclear parity. It is therefore highly questionable whether the security of the nuclear-weapon States—however defined—can be maintained on the basis of an arms race.

Nuclear weapons are the most serious threat to international security. One reason for this is that existing nuclear-weapon arsenals have acquired a role of their own in international relations. It is today possible that a grave accident or even a devastating war may be originated by the nuclear-weapon systems themselves, and the perceived threat they constitute against each other. This could be brought about, especially in a situation of high tension, by a pre-emptive strike or through an escalation from the conventional to the nuclear level.

It is therefore important to recall that the General Assembly, at its tenth special session in 1978, declared that effective measures of nuclear disarmament and the prevention of nuclear war have the highest priority, and urged all nuclear-weapon States, in particular those among them which possess the most important nuclear arsenals, to implement the measures set out in the Final Document in achieving these objectives. It is a matter of deep regret and concern that in the two years since then, no real progress has been achieved and that the nuclear-arms race continues unabated in both quantitative and qualitative terms.

When proceeding towards nuclear disarmament, it is essential to identify, as clearly as possible, the problems that will need to be confronted and resolved. In the first instance, the main problem is undoubtedly the very size and complexity of the arms race. According to the latest figures, the world today is spending every year the staggering amount of over $500 billion, that is to say, almost $1 million every minute on the arms race. Secondly, no other area of human activity involves research and development efforts comparable to what is wasted on the arms industry. Thirdly, there is obviously the lack of political will on the part of those concerned to accept the urgent necessity of moving towards nuclear disarmament. In a world still dominated by fear and distrust, the necessary political conditions or real disarmament seem far away. It should also be stressed that economic inequalities constitute a major destabilizing factor in international relations, and that disarmament cannot be undertaken with any success in a climate of grave and increasing economic inegalitarianism.

Moreover, there is also the undeniable role of the so-called military industrial complex, which obviously stands to benefit from the continuation and escalation of the arms race. It is imperative that the political leaders of the world control these forces rather than be controlled by them and thereby assume their responsibility for seeking increased international security at lower levels of armaments and through the eventual establishment of a security system that does not rely on the use or threat of the use of force.

The establishment of confidence among nations is crucial for international peace and security. Without confidence between States the political pre-conditions for reaching disarmament cannot be brought about. Disarmament measures may, in turn, enhance confidence among nations and the inter-relationship could thus be made to work in both directions. This does not detract, however, from the basic fact that confidence is essential for disarmament. This must be based not only on the assurance that agreed disarmament measures will be carried out with adequate verification but also on an attitude of mutual confidence. States, and in particular militarily-significant States, must not resort, in pursuit of their objectives, to force, threat of force or to interference in the internal affairs of States, as this inevitably destroys the degree of confidence necessary for the realization of progress in disarmament. Many also consider that a cut-off in arms spending and the reduction of military activities of alliances as well as a certain openness in military matters may enhance the confidence among all States.

History provides many examples of States that were adversaries but now enjoy peaceful relations, resting on a climate of confidence between themselves and characterized by peaceful co-operation and a high degree of interdependence. The spectrum of co-operation comprises not only trade and economic co-operation, but also cultural and scientific contacts, etc. Peaceful co-operation on a global scale among the countries of the world could lead to a state of affairs which would not only be characterized by the mere absence of armed conflict but also by the observation of an effective system of international peace and security.

There is thus a need that the alternative to the ongoing arms race be spelled out in its detailed consequences. Until those consequences have been generally accepted by all concerned, and in particular by the super-Powers who perceive the present system as working in their favour, the lack of political will to effect a decisive change will continue to persist. Thus, the road to nuclear disarmament is long and difficult.

The important question is, then, what can be done to bring about a decisive change, to create the necessary political will to bear on this situation and to embark on the search for a generally acceptable solution? The Final Document of the Tenth Special Session of the General Assembly outlines the broad objectives to be sought and the main methods to be used in the future search for international security and disarmament. Among these methods, the need must be stressed for adopting a comprehensive programme of disarmament which should be implemented in an integrated manner with the active involvement of all States. In this context, there is a continuing need to involve the United Nations as the main instrument not only for reaching international agreement in the field of disarmament but also for a broad development of international co-operation and interdependence.

In order to help create the necessary political will for disarmament the United Nations must continue to seek the more active involvement of its Members in the discussion and negotiation of concrete disarmament proposals. In addition, the clamour for lasting peace and real disarmament by the general public is an important political force that could be further mobilized by the United Nations through co-operation with non-governmental organizations and individuals. The United Nations must become more active in involving non-governmental organizations and individuals in the disarmament effort with a view to building strong world public opinion in matters of disarmament.

These approaches to disarmament represent by necessity a long-term effort, but it is urgent that effective steps be taken in this sense. As a result of the tenth special session, the United Nations is in the process of creating more effective instruments and machinery to provide both the information and the knowledge necessary for the official discussions and negotiations concerning disarmament and to aid the non-governmental organizations in their efforts of opinion making. In this context, the various United Nations studies in the field of disarmament as well as the questions of training and education have begun to receive attention and constitute important elements in the long-range objective of widening the understanding of these problems.

An important pre-requisite for the control and reduction of nuclear weapons is the availability of effective means to verify the compliance of States with the agreements concluded to this end. The nature of the verification methods will vary with the particular disarmament measure under consideration. One important example is the International Atomic Energy Agency safeguards system to verify non-diversion of fissionable materials from peaceful to military purposes. In all areas, however, the capability to monitor the implementation to disarmament is to be promoted with the involvement of all nuclear and non-nuclear countries. It would seem essential that the international community be empowered with the ability to verify reliable compliance with disarmament measures. In this context, the establishment of a disarmament organization, and of an international satellite monitoring agency, as well as of any other institution based on similar proposals is extremely relevant.

It is clear that the application of modern science to military purposes constitutes an important driving force for the nuclear arms race. Negotiations for nuclear disarmament must, therefore, seek ways and means of effectively controlling the contribution of scientific research and development to the arms race, particularly the nuclear arms race. It is in this context that a comprehensive test ban has been considered essential for many years.

Nuclear disarmament, if it is to be comprehensive and meaningful, will have to be pursued in a global context. It is to be understood that in the first stage, the two major nuclear-weapon States have to make the initial reductions in their nuclear arsenals and to effect substantive restraint in the qualitative development of nuclear-weapon systems. They should seek to achieve this objective in the framework of bilateral negotiations. Yet, if these negotiations are to produce a positive reaction from other nuclear and non-nuclear-weapon States, it is essential that the United States and the USSR should take into account the security interests of all States and keep the Committee on Disarmament and other relevant bodies closely informed of the progress in their bilateral negotiations, the areas of agreement and disagreement, etc. This is equally true of nuclear disarmament, which must be pursued at all levels in every region.

So far, the Strategic Arms Limitation Talks between the two super-Powers have come to be based on the premise of nuclear parity and within the framework of a continued reliance on a balance of mutual deterrence. The general belief is that, even within their approach, it could be possible to find a new level of parity at a much lower level of armaments through reductions in the enormous numbers of strategic and tactical nuclear weapons that exist. The agreements within SALT have, as yet, not led to any such reductions and have failed to put a cap on the arms race.

Another difficulty lies in the concept of parity itself. The weapon systems of the two super-Powers are in fact asymmetrical in that they are not exactly similar in terms of operation, power or effectiveness. Although this seems to be an accepted state of affairs so far as the two super-Powers are concerned, China and France have taken the position that they would be prepared to participate in the strategic arms negotiations only when the super-Power arsenals had been considerably reduced.

It is, therefore, apparent that the two super-Powers will be constantly urged to take the initial steps to halt and reverse their mutual escalations, and to make the greatest contribution to the process of nuclear disarmament. The world community must press for a speedier and more substantive result of the SALT negotiations. Simultaneously, in view of the link between the strategic and tactical forces of the two opposing military blocs, attention must turn to restraining and reversing the deployment of theatre nuclear forces in Europe. This effort, in turn, will require that the level of conventional forces of the negotiating parties be considered.

There is a growing concern over the possible increase in the number of nuclear-weapon States that may take place overtly or covertly. This problem requires the serious attention of the world community because it represents a development in a direction opposite to that of nuclear disarmament. At the same time there should be even stronger efforts to curb the vertical proliferation of nuclear weapons. The world community has discovered that the problem of horizontal proliferation involves difficulties comparable to those of vertical non-proliferation. There are questions of energy security, transfer of technology and nuclear safeguards, to give just some examples. The attitude of those nuclear-weapon States which emphasize only horizontal non-proliferation while resorting to political and military "realities" as excuses for the slow pace of curbing the nuclear arms race does not contribute to the cause of mutual confidence-building within the international community.

The success of negotiations on the reduction of nuclear weapons in a regional context may sometimes depend on the success of the bilateral efforts of the two super-Powers and their allies. But, increasingly, the relationship between strategic, "theatre" and tactical nuclear weapons will need to be taken into account if significant progress is to be made towards the goal of nuclear disarmament. In many cases, the reduction of nuclear weapons will require that regional security conditions be taken into account. Among these, the size and military power of the various States and groups of States concerned would form a relevant factor. Thus, in some cases a regional approach may be followed, independently of or in parallel with a bilateral one.

However, regional situations vary. In certain areas nuclear weapons are deployed on the territories of nuclear-weapon States as well as non-nuclear-weapon States allied to the nuclear Powers. Nuclear weapons are also deployed on surface ships and submarines in various sea areas adjacent both to areas where nuclear weapons exist and others which are free of them. There are regions free of nuclear weapons and all efforts must be made to maintain this particular status. Finally, the creation of further nuclear-weapon-free zones pursued at the regional level, on the basis of arrangements freely arrived at between the States concerned, should be strongly encouraged.

Even if the road to nuclear disarmament is a long and difficult one, there is no alternative. Peace requires the prevention of the danger of a nuclear war. If nuclear disarmament is to become a reality, the commitment to mutual deterrence through a balance of terror must be discarded. The concept of the maintenance of world peace, stability and balance through the process of deterrence is perhaps the most dangerous collective fallacy that exists. This report has detailed the massive and lethal quantum of nuclear weapons that exist in the world and the rate of their daily accumulation: it has indicated the devastating effects and consequences of even a fractional utilization of these vast stockpiles. The report has also described the so-called tactical nuclear weapons with their consequent destructive effects. But it must be emphasized that even if one such weapon was ever used in war, it could become the immediate and inevitable prelude to a total nuclear holocaust. The present report has attempted to discuss the control systems that currently exist, but there is no conviction of their total efficacy despite the sophistication that is attributed to these systems by their possessors. The very real prospects of nuclear proliferation—in the absence of the nuclear Powers' ability to halt and reverse their arms race *inter se*—will inevitably confront the world with a multidimensional problem of the most serious nature.

So long as reliance continues to be placed upon the concept of the balance of nuclear deterrence as a method for maintaining peace, the prospects for the future will always remains dark, menacing and as uncertain as the fragile assumptions upon which they are based. Fortunately, this is not the only alternative that is available to mankind. We have, in the United Nations, an institution which should be utilized for all the purposes and stages that are relevant to the process of disarmament—negotiation, agreement, implementation, verification and ratification where necessary. What is needed is the creation of a strong public opinion which should, in time, create the political will among all States to transfer their security reliance from the nuclear-weapon system to another universally accepted system. Only a system of international security based on the observation of the principles of the United Nations Charter and of other universally accepted instruments of international law can provide a mutually acceptable basis of security. This must therefore be the goal on the road to nuclear disarmament. The Charter and nuclear weapons date their existence from the same time. The future road should point to a full reliance on the Charter and to the elimination of all nuclear weapons.

Appendix I

Technical Description of Nuclear-Weapon Effects

Air blast and effects
Air blast

Immediately after a nuclear fission (or fusion) process, nuclear constituents are ejected with tremendous velocities. Through collision and other more complicated processes most of these particles are stopped within a very short distance and their energy is eventually transferred to the surrounding air. This will at some distance from the point of burst manifest itself as a sharp increase in air pressure called static overpressure accompanied by high winds called dynamic overpressure. In older texts, these overpressures are usually given in atmospheres (atm) or pounds per square inch (PSI). The new international unit is called megapascal (MPa; 1 MPa is approximately equal to 10 atm or 145 PSI). To facilitate the reading of this appendix, overpressure will be given in all three units.

Compared to the blast of a large chemical explosion, the duration of that from a nuclear explosion is considerably longer except for very small-yield weapons—of the order of 1 second for a 20 kt. burst and several seconds for a 1 Mt. burst. Since the damage caused by blast increases with the duration as well as the magnitude of the static and dynamic overpressures, a nuclear explosion is more devastating than a chemical blast at a distance where both would have the same peak overpressure.

All nuclear air bursts—regardless of the design of the weapon—will release a large portion of their total energy as blast. For a "standard" weapon this will amount to approximately 50 per cent. Hence, this is a major cause of damage.

Intuitively one might believe that the strongest blast would be produced at a given distance from ground zero when the nuclear weapon is detonated as a surface explosion. Due to reflections of the air shock wave against the ground, however, this is not true. For a given weapon yield and a given level of blast overpressure, there is always a particular height of burst that maximizes the area covered by at least that overpressure. This height of burst varies with the level of overpressure chosen. Hence if the aim is to optimize destruction of a solidly built industrial section, the height of burst should be somewhat lower than if maximum destruction of a residential area is intended.

With increasing height of burst the overpressure that reaches the ground decreases rapidly. As the height of the burst is lowered under the optimization height for some overpressure, the area covered by that overpressure decreases somewhat. In the immediate vicinity of ground zero, however, blast will become increasingly stronger as the air burst gradually turns into a surface burst. Much of the air shock will be transformed to a ground shock and eventually a crater will be formed. To form a crater, melting and vaporization of the ground due to the fireball are, however, essential in addition to blast. Severe damage to heavily fortified underground structures such as missile silos is in general believed to require surface or subsurface bursts.[58]

Modifying factors

The contour covered by overpressure of some particular magnitude is usually represented as a circle. In actuality there are a number of modifying factors, which would destroy this idealized shape. Most important among these are terrain effects such as hills, trees or buildings in a populated area. Large hilly land, for instance, will increase air blast effects in some areas and decrease them in others. These shielding effects will not, however, be dependent upon line of sight considerations, since the blast will "bend around corners", "bend over tops", enter "through small holes", etc. Hence no space which is directly connected with the atmosphere one way or another will escape the overpressure. When blast is reflected against a mountain side, a wall—exterior or interior—of a house or a similar object, the result will sometimes be a local increase, sometimes a decrease. The overpressure at the reflecting surface might reach several times the peak value of the incident blast wave. The exact overpressure patterns will hence be quite complicated in a built-up area or a hilly, forested landscape.

Damage caused by air blast

When discussing effects of air blast it is customary to distinguish between direct and indirect damage. Direct damage is, for instance, collapse of walls and roofs due to the fact that one side of these surfaces experiences a tremendous increase in the static overpressure whereas the other does not. Direct damage to objects such as trees in a forest, telephone poles and metal sheet constructions is mainly caused by the strong winds. Direct damage to humans could consist of eardrum rupture at moderate overpressure and in addition hemorrhage of the lungs at higher overpressures. Still higher overpressures would cause air to be forced into the veins through the lungs resulting in death within a few minutes. Generally speaking, a human being can withstand much higher pressures without fatal direct injuries than those required to severely damage even very solid buildings. Indirect damage, caused by collapsing buildings, glass fragments and other debris flying in the air or high winds dragging people into solid objects, is a much more likely mechanism for producing blast injuries and fatalities, since this can occur at distances from ground zero when the direct blast damage is negligible for humans. As little as 0.015-0.02 MPa (0.15-0.20 atm or 2-3 PSI) could be expected to blow people out of modern office buildings, for instance.

Considering the fact that an attacked area will in general contain objects of various resistance to blast such as buildings more or less solidly constructed, trees of various sizes and kinds in a forest and local variations in the overpressures due to terrain effects, it is clear that the damage picture from blast will in most cases look very complex. Apart from a totally demolished region around ground zero for a low altitude air burst, some objects closer to ground zero such as bridges or reinforced concrete buildings might be left moderately damaged whereas other objects further away, such as buildings of lighter construction, will have collapsed completely. Under these circumstances and having in mind the random nature of indirect blast injuries, it is clearly impossible to give a precise "distance of survival" from blast for human beings from a nuclear burst of some particular yield and height. For rough estimates some studies assume that the number of unprotected people in a populated area who survive in an area covered by at least 0.035 MPa (0.35 atm or 5 PSI) equals the number of people killed in areas receiving less than that overpressure. Hence blast fatalities are considered to be everybody inside 0.035 MPa circle. For military personnel and equipment or people in shelters other overpressure damage criteria—depending on the protection assumed—of course have to be assumed.

Thermal radiation and its effects
Thermal radiation

About 35 per cent of the total energy released in an air burst and about 25 per cent of that in a surface burst will be emitted as thermal radiation (light and heat) within the first minute following the explosion. Most of this energy will be released in the first few seconds.

The composition of this thermal radiation is quite similar to that of the sun with some ultraviolet but mostly visible and infra-red light. Hence the first noticeable sign that a nuclear air burst has taken place will to an observer at some distance be a very bright flash or "lightning" and—depending on the distance—a more or less intense wave of heat. For a surface burst, the thermal radiation that reaches an object at some distance from ground zero will be less than for a low air burst since part of the thermal energy of a surface burst is absorbed by the earth, rock or water at ground zero, and part of it is shielded by surrounding terrain irregularities. For a high altitude burst, i.e. above 30 km. (100,000 ft.), thermal effects on the ground can be ignored, except for very high

Figure A:1 The "Optimum Height of Burst" Concept

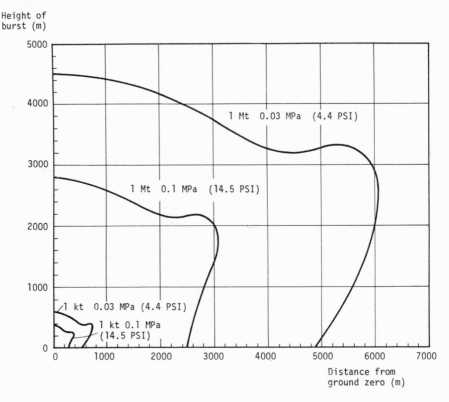

Height of
burst (m)

5000

4000

1 Mt 0.03 MPa (4.4 PSI)

3000

1 Mt 0.1 MPa (14.5 PSI)

2000

1000

1 kt 0.03 MPa (4.4 PSI)

1 kt 0.1 MPa
(14.5 PSI)

0

0   1000   2000   3000   4000   5000   6000   7000

Distance from
ground zero (m)

Due to shock reflection at the ground, the area covered by at least a given over-pressure depends on height of burst as well as on weapon yield. This is illustrated for two different overpressures and two different yields. It can be seen that a 1 Mt surface burst will give a 0.03 MPa at about 4900 m distance from ground zero, while the same explosion 2500 m above will give that overpressure at just over 6000 m ground zero distance.

yield weapons of the order of 10 Mt. or more.

Weather and terrain conditions will affect the amount of thermal energy reflected or absorbed by the atmosphere considerably. Fog, smoke or heavy clouds will substantially reduce the amount of thermal radiation that under clear atmospheric conditions would reach an object. On the other hand reflecting surfaces, such as snow or ice, will enhance thermal radiation. We finally note here that for underground or underwater bursts thermal energy will only be effective very close to the fireball, since if there is no surface breakthrough the heat will rapidly by absorbed by the surrounding earth or water.

Damage caused by thermal radiation

Under clear or fairly clear atmospheric conditions, human beings will receive second-degree burn injuries to unprotected skin at a considerable distance from ground zero. An indication of what these distances might be is given by figure A2. Second-degree burns over 30 per cent of the body will result in serious shock and in general require medical treatment within hours for survival. Untreated third-degree burns will prove fatal if about 25 per cent of the skin area has been damaged. Clothes will provide some protection depending on the thickness and material of the fabric, but will eventually transport heat through to the skin and (or) catch fire.

Under most circumstances, hands and faces are those parts of the body that will be directly exposed for unwarned unprotected humans. In addition to the risk of skin burns, the eyes are quite sensitive to the light emitted. A 1 Mt. explosion could cause flash blindness at 20 km. (13 miles) in daytime and 85 km. (53 miles) at nighttime, and retinal burns at somewhat shorter distances. While the eyesight will eventually return after flash blindness, the loss of it in a critical situation, such as driving a car, could well cause severe accidents. Even if the injuries are not too severe in a medical sense, burned face and hands would be a substantial handicap in the aftermath of a nuclear explosion. Depending on the circumstances, both of these types of injuries might affect a huge number of people due to the vast areas involved.

Fires

In addition to causing direct (flash) burns and flash blindness, thermal radiation will ignite combustible materials. These might consist of curtains, rugs, beds and furniture inside buildings as windowglass will not stop thermal radiation noticeably. Consequently, extensive fires inside buildings could be expected to result, even at distances where the blast does not cause too much damage. Depending on the weather, moisture at the ground, etc., paper and plastic litter, dry wood, dry grass and leaves would be ignited over a more or less large area. It is generally believed, however, that the density of such combustible materials in many sections of urban areas in today's industrial society is not sufficient to cause extensive fires. A large uncertainty is the interaction between blast and

Figure A:2. Distances for Flash Burns

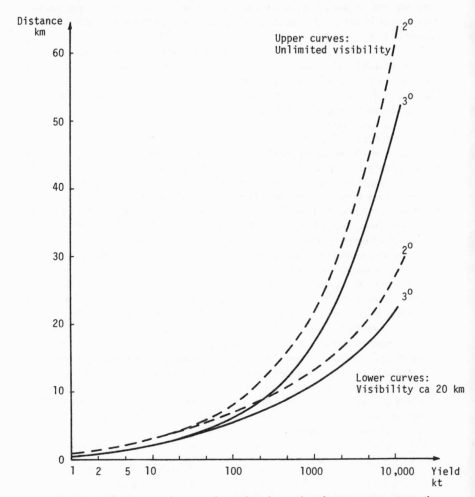

The distance from ground zero where the thermal radiation may cause skin burns depends strongly on both yield and atmospheric conditions. The chart shows, as a function of yield, the theoretically calculated distance for second- and third-degree burns in a clear atmosphere and in a virtually empty space.

fire. On one hand blast will extinguish many points of fire caused by thermal radiation, but on the other hand it will increase the density of combustible materials in certain areas by producing debris and thus increase the risk for a later spread of fire.

Another source of fires in an urban area will be blast damage to stoves, water heaters, furnaces, electrical circuits and gas lines. And when nuclear weapons are used over forested areas—e.g., on a battlefield—the combination of forest blowdown through blast and possible forest fires in dry weather could create hazardous conditions for people in such areas.

The individual fires—caused by thermal ignition or indirectly through blast— might under certain circumstances merge into a mass fire over a large area. These could then be of two kinds: a firestorm with high winds rushing inwards creating extremely high temperatures or a "conflagration", i.e. a moving firefront driven by ambient winds. In addition to Hiroshima, well-known examples of firestorms are those of Dresden, Hamburg and Tokyo caused by conventional bombing in the Second World War. People caught in these often did not survive even in shelters, due to heat and asphyxiation.

Even if a firestorm does not develop, many people in urban areas—and possibly forests—who might otherwise have survived could be trapped by blast debris, leg injuries, unconsciousness from head injuries and hence die due to their inability to escape from even a slowly developing fire. It has been estimated that about 50 per cent of the casualties in Hiroshima resulted from direct or indirect burn injuries. Close to two thirds of those who survived for a few days and then died are reported to have been badly burned. The high incidence of burn injuries and casualties in Hiroshima was caused by a number of coinciding factors, such as a warm clear day, the time of explosion taking place in the morning with many people being outdoors, etc., favouring burn injuries. Even so, these types of injuries should, unless the circumstances are exceptional, be regarded as a very likely major cause of casualties whenever there is a nuclear explosion over or in the vicinity of an urban area. This is particularly true for larger-yield weapons, where the area covered by thermal radiation intense enough to cause third-degree burns or ignite easily inflammable material is considerably larger than that covered by hazardous blast or initial nuclear radiation.

The electromagnetic pulse and its effects

A nuclear explosion—just as lightning—generates a sharp and short electromagnetic pulse (EMP) but with a higher intensity and shorter rise time. The mechanisms responsible for producing electromagnetic waves in the form of EMP are rather complicated, but are in essence due to the absorption of some of the nuclear high energy gamma rays which are immediately released by the nuclear reactions at the moment of explosion. In the absorption processes, electrons are torn away from the surrounding media leaving behind electrically charged atoms (ions). It is, roughly speaking, this rapid separation of electrons from the atoms that generates the electromagnetic pulse, which will then propagate outwards with the velocity of light.

Although the relative amount of energy from a nuclear explosion released as EMP is less than 0.01 per cent of the total, that is still a considerable amount in absolute terms. While the EMP waves are qualitatively similar to those produced by a radio (or TV) transmitter, they differ in two important respects. First, EMP contains electromagnetic waves of all frequencies from a very low to a very high range, whereas a radio transmitter sends at one or a few frequencies. Secondly, the rise time and duration of an EMP is extremely short—in fact the rise time is about 100 times shorter than the EMP produced by ordinary lightning. Hence an EMP consists of very strong electromagnetic fields—of the order of a million times those generated by a radio transmitter—with a very rapid rise (and fall) of the fields. Because of the short rise time of the EMP, devices designed to protect electrical and electronic equipment against lightning will often be inadequate for protection against the effects of nuclear EMP.

When the height of burst is varied for some given explosion, the strength of the EMP signal received at some given distance from ground zero will vary considerably. Surface or low air bursts of a weapon of moderate size will generate EMP that may have harmful effects on electrical and electronic equipment out to a distance of about 3-10 km. (2 to 6 miles) from ground zero, depending on the explosion yield and the equipment sensitivity. The strength of the EMP at the ground will then decrease with increasing height of burst up to an altitude of ca. 10 to 15 km. (35,000 to 50,000 ft.). When bursts occur at still higher altitudes, a strong EMP will again be experienced on the ground. This is due to the combined effects of atmospheric density variation with altitude and the geomagnetic field. This EMP covers a wide area, since it extends outwards in all directions as far as the line-of-sight from the burst point. A nuclear explosion at an altitude of 80 km. would affect a circular area with a radius of about 1,000 km. and an altitude of 160 km. (100 miles) would produce effects over a circular area with a radius of about 1,500 km. (900 miles). Thus a high altitude burst might cause EMP damage at ground where all other effects (except possibly flash blindness at night) would be negligible.

The EMP energy is collected in antennae—or objects serving as unintentional antennae—just as the energy of ordinary radio waves. Depending on the length and orientation of the antenna—as well as whether it is in the air, on or slightly under the ground—it will collect more or less EMP energy. This energy might then be transported—sometimes over large distances—to electrical or electronic systems connected to its ends. The larger the antenna—or unintended antenna, such as telephone or electrical wire—the more EMP energy it will collect.

At the end of a conductor, the pulse might cause burnout of a sensitive electronic component such as an LSI circuit, or some other component of a system

Figure A:3. High Altitude EMP

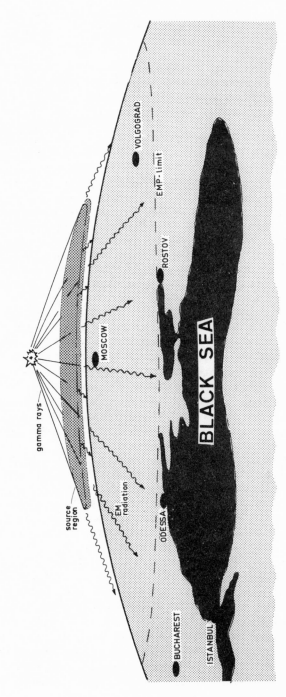

201

A nuclear explosion at, say, 100 km above the earth will create EMP phenomena within a 1200 km circle. If, for instance, Moscow were chosen as ground zero, the EMP disturbance would reach from the Kola Peninsula to the Black Sea. It would also cover parts of Finland, Poland, and Romania. (The heights of the burst and the source region are greatly exaggerated in comparison to the curvature of the earth.)

and hence cause malfunctioning or breakdown of the entire system. Through a chain reaction, electrical power and telephone networks might collapse although the uncertainty in this field is large.

Initial nuclear radiation

The essential difference between a nuclear and large conventional (chemical) explosion with regard to blast and thermal radiation is one of magnitude. Differences in effects merely reflect differences in amount of energy released. There are, however, consequences of a nuclear burst that do not have any counterpart in a conventional explosion: the immediate release of nuclear radiation and the creation of radioactive particles which will go on emitting nuclear radiation for a long time. It is customary to separate this radiation into two parts—that emitted within one minute around the burst point and that caused by the return of radioactive particles (fallout) over an extended period of time to the ground. The former is referred to as initial nuclear radiation and the time of one minute is chosen because after this period the "mushroom cloud" containing most of the radioactive particles for an air burst will have risen to a height from which the radiation can reach the ground in negligible amounts only.

The initial nuclear radiation—most of which will be released in the first seconds following a nuclear explosion—consists essentially of fast neutrons and gamma rays. Although part of this radiation will be absorbed by the weapon material itself, colossal amounts will in general escape to represent a significant hazard to living organisms and radiation-sensitive electronic systems. The initial (and residual) radiation can be varied within a considerable range for weapons of the same total yield. Initial radiation neutrons will furthermore induce some radioactivity in the soil around ground zero, the extent of which largely depends upon the chemical composition of the soil.

The most important quantity for assessing radiation injury or damage is called "dose", which is the amount of radiation energy absorbed per unit mass of the absorbing material. Dose levels associated with various degrees of radiation injury in humans and other living organisms are discussed later in this appendix.

When travelling in the air, radiation will be attenuated rapidly with increasing distance from ground zero. Thus, the difference between distances where a lethal dose and a negligible dose of initial radiation will be received is fairly small. Generally speaking about 400 to 600 m. (0.25-0.40 mile) will reduce the dose by a factor of 10. Hence 800 to 1,200 m. (0.5-0.8 mile) will reduce it by about a factor of 100. This distance varies somewhat with the yield and the distance from the weapon, being larger for larger-yield weapons. Some dose-distance relationships are indicated in figure A:4.

As the height of burst increases from a low air burst to a high air burst, the amount of radiation reaching the ground rapidly diminishes. A 1 Mt. burst at an altitude of 5 km. (3 miles) would give a negligible dose at ground zero and so would a 100 kt. burst at an altitude of roughly 4 km. (2.5 miles).

Figure A:4. Initial Radiation Dose vs. Ground Zero Distance

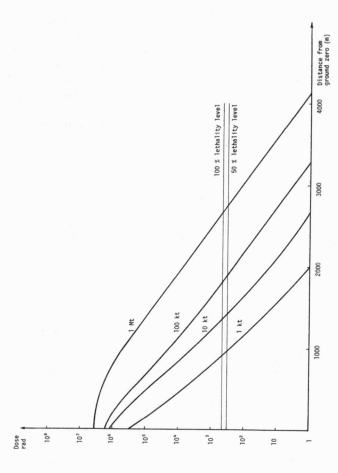

The rapid attenuation with distance of the initial radiation is clearly seen. The curves have been calculated for the following heights of burst: 1 kt: 100 m; 10 kt: 215 m; 100 kt: 465 m; 1 Mt: 1000 m. Peculiarities in the 1 Mt curve are due to geometry factors, to the influence of the fusion component on radiation and to rarefaction of the ambient air which decreases attenuation.

In addition to living organisms, electronic components could be quite sensitive to initial radiation. While older type equipment is resistant even to high doses, modern large-scale integrated (LSI) circuits might malfunction or break down at quite low doses. The reason for this is that even though the probability of damaging one element in the circuit is low, the circuit is composed of so many interacting units that the resulting probability of malfunction or breakdown becomes rather high. Thyristors are also very sensitive to rapidly delivered radiation doses. Electronic systems exposed to low or medium yield detonations might be affected by initial radiation while at the same time having a chance of surviving the other damaging effects of the nuclear burst. Such systems could, for instance, be part of some military equipment.

Ionizing radiation will penetrate any material and gradually undergo absorption. Effective protection therefore implies thick and heavy layers of material. As a rule of thumb, the heavier the material the better it absorbs radiation, although other criteria apply to neutrons.

Residual radiation (fallout)

In addition to the initial radiation of gamma rays and neutrons, a large amount of radioactive elements will also be produced by fission processes and possibly other neutron reactions in the weapons material. These elements will adhere to particles formed from weapon debris and, in the case of a land surface burst, also from ground material. The radioactivity associated with such particles is called residual radiation. For a detonation at or close to the surface, initially released neutrons will induce radioactivity in the ground adding to the fission and weapon debris; residual radiation as some ground material will be drawn into the fireball. Since a fusion reaction will not produce any radioactive rest products, its contribution to residual radiation will be caused only by neutron-induced activity.

Radioactive elements will lose their radioactivity with time due to "decay". The rate of decay varies from a fraction of a second to many years, depending on the element considered. Two important elements, strontium-99 and cesium-137, for instance, will retain half of their radioactivity after about 30 years, and hence cause long-term health hazards. Carbon-14, which is formed from the nitrogen in the atmosphere when irradiated with neutrons, has a half-life of about 5,800 years and will thus continue to give small radiation doses to many generations.

Particles containing residual radiation are usually referred to as fallout. The later the fallout reaches the ground, the less hazardous it is, due to the decay of the radioactivity. Early fallout results only for a surface or very low air burst, and hence these types will have far more serious consequences than an air burst.

A surface burst results in the creation of large and heavy radioactive particles which will fall down within minutes around ground zero. Other lighter and smaller particles, however, will follow the fireball and cloud further up, drift with the winds and then fall down in a plume-like area in the general direction of persisting winds. While these particles are smaller than those closer to ground zero, they will on a smooth surface still be visible as dust whenever fallout is sufficient to represent a significant immediate hazard. This fallout will start coming down within less than an hour and keep falling for about a day or two depending on the distance from ground zero. The smallest particles, finally, will be ejected into the stratosphere—at least for a weapon of large yield—and remain there for months or years, before returning to the ground again. An air burst on the other hand, i.e. a burst where the fireball is well above the ground, will cause essentially all residual radiation particles to ascend with the fireball and mushroom cloud. Eventually they will spread out and return to the ground as dilute world-wide fallout.

There are a number of factors deciding the extent and intensity of fallout, the most important of which are meteorological conditions. If there is no steady wind, or if the winds are blowing in different directions at different altitudes, the fallout area will have a very complicated shape with possible "hot spots", essentially impossible to predict with any accuracy in advance. In rainy or snowy weather an air burst below the clouds which would otherwise have caused negligible fallout could produce considerable and unpredictable local fallout, since radioactive particles will reach the ground through rain (or snow). The latter mechanism is of more relative significance for small-yield weapons than for those of large yield, however.

The most important process for an area to become inhabitable again is the natural decay of radioactivity. Weathering, i.e. the effects of rain and wind, will speed up the time required for some area to reach a state of "acceptable" radiation intensity, since this process will remove radioactive particles into water, soil, etc., where they will in general be less hazardous than on the ground. Decontamination, finally, will contribute to diminishing the intensity in limited areas if properly executed. Even so, heavily contaminated areas will be uninhabitable for tens of years or more, if present standards of radiation safety are to be maintained.

Radiation injuries

Nuclear radiation will always inflict some damage to biological tissue. Generally speaking, this damage and the resulting radiation injury to the organism will be the more severe, the larger the radiation dose. The definition of "dose" and related concepts as well as their units are given in table A.1.

Almost all of the initial radiation dose will be received from high intensity radiation released within seconds in the immediate vicinity of the burst. Large doses associated with early fallout will on the other hand be caused by lower intensity radiation received under a long period of time—from hours up to days and in some cases even months. A slowly accumulated dose is generally considered less harmful than an equally large instantaneous dose, due to recovery mechanisms. No distinction between these cases will be upheld here, however.

Figure A:5. Fallout Patterns

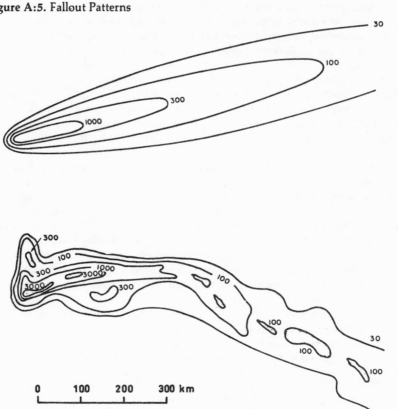

The upper part of the figure shows an idealized set of dose-rate contours. Numbers are dose-rates in rad/h at one hour after the explosion, and the size of the contours corresponds to a 10 Mt, 50-percent fission surface burst and a 50 km/h effective wind speed. The lower part is hypothetical picture of how the same fallout pattern might look in reality. Note the change in overall direction of the pattern. (From: *Effects of Nuclear Weapons*, Washington 1977)

For humans, animals and plants, absorbed radiation will damage cells, which may result in injuries to the particular organs. The resulting injury to the biological individual will vary, depending on the species, the magnitude and composition of the dose and on age and general condition of the irradiated individual.

While the major danger connected with high intensity fallout radiation arises from particles outside the body emitting gamma rays, radioactive material will also enter the body through breathing, eating and drinking. It is in this regard of particular importance to prevent radioactive iodine 131 from entering the body within the first weeks or so, especially for children, since it will be concentrated in the thyroid glands with subsequent high risks of contracting thyroid cancer. Of particular importance are also strontium-90 and cesium-137. Strontium will primarily enter the body through the milk and meat of grazing cattle, sheep, etc., whereas cesium is absorbed by root systems of vegetables and other plants, and will reach the body by consumption of these types of foods. While strontium will be deposited in the bone, causing possible skeleton cancer, leukaemia, etc., cesium will be distributed roughly evenly throughout the body. Plutonium has been mentioned as a possible hazard, but is generally not considered to be among the most dangerous constituents released in a nuclear explosion.

When discussing human radiation injuries three categories can be identified: acute radiation injuries, increased probability of late cancer and genetic (hereditary) effects. In what follows, whole body irradiation is always implied unless otherwise stated, and the dose values indicated are average whole body doses. These are lower by about a factor 0.7 than superficial doses given in some other publications (cf. table A.1). No other injury is assumed.

Acute radiation injuries

Below a dose of 100 rad, essentially no clinical symptoms will be experienced. Doses in the range 100 to 200 rad would cause acute radiation sickness, characterized by nausea, vomiting, diarrhoea and fatigue to a small fraction of an exposed population at the lower end of the interval and to the majority in the upper end. Damage to blood cells will result in lowered resistance to infections and delayed recovery from other injuries. In the interval 200 to 400 rad, about 5 to 10 per cent fatalities would result after a month in the lower range and 90 per cent or more are expected to become fatalities at the upper range. The 50 per cent fatality dose is about 300 rad. Radiation sickness would in the middle and upper part of this interval be intense and those who recover would do so only after several months. Medical treatment is already in peacetime of marginal utility and should not be expected to be of any help in a situation comprising mass radiation injuries, except in the form of palliative treatment. Doses above 450 rad should be considered lethal and death will generally occur within a few weeks. At very high doses (thousands of rads) damage to the central nervous system will cause convulsions, tremor, ataxia and lethargy, followed by death within 1 to 48 hours.

Table A.1 Some quantities and units related to ionizing radiation

Quantity	Definition	Traditional unit	SI unit	Remarks
Exposure	Amount of ionization produced by gamma or X-rays per unit mass of dry air	roentgen (R)	coulomb per kilogram (C/kg) $1 \text{ C/kg} = 3{,}876 \text{ R}$	
Intensity or exposure rate	Exposure per unit time	roentgen per hour (R/h) or roentgen per second (R/s)	ampere per kilogram (A/kg) $1 \text{ A/kg} = 3{,}876 \text{ R/s}$	
Dose (absorbed dose)	Amount of energy absorbed per unit mass of absorber	rad $1 \text{ rad} = 0.01 \text{ J/kg}$	gray (Gy) $1 \text{ Gy} = 1 \text{ J/kg} = 100 \text{ rad}$	An exposure of 1 R is equivalent to a dose of about 0.9 rad in air or superficial tissue and about 0.7 rad in mid-tissue (average whole body dose).
Dose rate	Dose per unit time	rad per hour (rad/h) or rad per second (rad/s)	gray per second (Gy/s) $1 \text{ Gy/s} = 100 \text{ rad/s}$	
Dose equivalent	Dose calculated with regard to the relative biological effects of different types of radiation	rem	sievert (Sv)	This quantity is the basis of civilian (peacetime) standards for radiation protection. For most of the radiation from a nuclear burst, dose equivalents in rem are approximately equal to doses in rad.

Radiation will affect mammals and birds in a way similar to humans. There are, however, some lower species of animals that will survive doses of thousands of rads. The same holds true for most plants.

Induced late cancer

It is well known that large doses of radiation will increase the probability of contracting late cancer. However, compared to the natural frequency of cancer, small doses (i.e. in the range of 10 rad or less) have so far added statistically insignificant or undetectable increases to the natural frequency of cancer. This does not mean that doses in this range are harmless, and for protection purposes a linear relationship between doses and probability of contracting late cancer is usually assumed for low doses. According to the International Commission on Radiological Protection (ICRP),[59] there would be one to two cases of lethal cancer per 10,000 manrad. (The manrad is the unit for "collective dose", defined as the product of average dose and the number of people who have received that dose. Hence 10,000 manrad would be for instance 1 rad to 10,000 people, 10 rad to 1,000 people, etc.)

Genetic effects

The genetic effects considered here are hereditary defects that will be manifest only in future generations. They are caused by radiation-induced changes in the gonad cells. These defects might consist of lowered fertility, spontaneous abortion, stillborn children, children born with malformations or nonspecific constitutional weaknesses. To assess any precise relationship between radiation doses and frequencies of genetic damage is difficult. It is, however, believed to be of about the same order of magnitude as that of radiation-induced cancer. According to ICRP, the total risk for serious genetic defects is estimated at one case in 10,000 manrad. About half of these defects will show up in the first two generations following the irradiated parents.

Combined injuries and synergism in general

The preceding discussions have, in essence, been restricted to one effect at a time, and interactions of various effects have largely been disregarded. Such interactions will occur, however, and generally speaking they are expected to be synergic, which means that a combination of weapons effects will produce a more severe result than the sum of the injuries or damage caused by each single effect.

For study purposes, immediate casualties from a nuclear explosion can be treated as caused by one dominating effect—i.e. the one having the largest lethal radius with respect to yield, height-of-burst, degree of protection, etc. In every situation, however, there will be a zone where one effect by itself would not cause large numbers of fatalities but where many people might still succumb due to a combination of injuries. This was observed in humans after the 1945 bombings in Japan, and later animal experiments have contributed to the under-

standing of the biological mechanisms involved. These are related to the depletion, caused by ionizing radiation, of certain corpuscles in the blood which produces a state of general weakness and, in particular, a degradation of the
immunological defence in the body.

Most serious seems to be a combination of thermal burns and radiation. As
low a dose as 100 rad could be prohibitive to the body's own capacity for
recovery from thermal burns and might hence cause death in cases where the
person would otherwise have recovered from his burns. A similar process results
when radiation is combined with a mechanical injury from blast such as a punc-
ture wound from flying glass or wood, broken bones, cuts and internal injuries.
At a dose of 200 rad such wounds might be fatal—through infection or loss of
blood—where they would otherwise have healed. The general susceptibility to
infections, which may persist for many months, will prove a serious complica-
tion even in cases of rather slight injuries, especially when medical care is
unavailable.

Combination injuries with a radiation component will be most frequent after
explosions with low to intermediate yields (up to some tens of kilotons). This is
due to the fact that the relative importance of various weapons effects at any
given distance is dependent on yield.

The stress on the body from combined mechanical and thermal injuries would
probably also cause casualties where a person might otherwise have survived
either of these two injuries. This could be expected to be quite a frequent combination for larger-yield weapons—100 kt. or more—detonated as air bursts,
since people within range of harmful initial radiation doses will have little or no
probability of surviving blast and thermal effects.

In addition to synergisms of a purely biological type, combinations of human
injuries and material damage may be expected to aggravate the post-attack situation at all levels, from the individual up to society as a whole. An example of a
synergic mechanism of this kind would be immobility of people caused by
mechanical injuries or trapping in partly collapsed buildings resulting in inability to escape developing fires. Although interactions of this type will occur in
any war and are not specific to a nuclear situation, they could be expected to be
very frequent after a nuclear attack. For this reason, the number of victims
within a month after a nuclear strike or so could easily be underestimated.

Appendix II

"Security Assurances" by the Nuclear-Weapon States as Presented to the Committee on Disarmament in 1980

China

"Complete prohibition and total destruction of nuclear weapons are essential for the elimination of nuclear war and nuclear threats. We are aware that its realization is no easy matter. This being the case, we hold that the nuclear-weapon States should at least undertake not to use or threaten to use nuclear weapons against the non-nuclear-weapon States and nuclear-free zones. On its own initiative and unilaterally, China long ago declared that at no time and in no circumstances would it be the first to use nuclear weapons". (CD/133)

France

"To negotiate with nuclear-free zones participants in order to contract effective and binding commitments, as appropriate, precluding any use or threat of use of nuclear weapons against the States of these zones". (CD/139)

Soviet Union

"To offer a binding commitment in a new international convention not to use or threaten to use nuclear weapons against non-nuclear States parties to such a convention which renounce the production and acquisition of nuclear weapons and which have no nuclear weapons in their territory or under their jurisdiction or control and to consult whenever any party to the convention has reason to believe that the actions of any other party are in violation of this commitment".

"The Soviet Union, for its part, wishes to state as emphatically as it can that we are against the use of nuclear weapons, that only extraordinary circumstances, only aggression against our country or its allies by another nuclear Power, could compel us to have recourse to that extreme means of self-defence. The Soviet Union is doing and will do all in its power to prevent the outbreak of a nuclear war and to protect the peoples from becoming the victims of nuclear

211

strikes, whether initial or retaliatory. This is our steadfast policy, and we shall act in accordance with it".

"I wish also solemnly to declare that the Soviet Union will never use nuclear weapons against those States which renounce the production and acquisition of such weapons and do not have them on their territory". (CD/139)

United Kingdom

"Not to use nuclear weapons against States which are parties to the non-proliferation Treaty or other internationally binding commitments not to manufacture or acquire nuclear explosive devices except in the case of an attack on the United Kingdom, its dependent territories, its armed forces or its allies by such States in association or alliance with a nuclear-weapon State". (CD/139)

United States

"Not to use nuclear weapons against any non-nuclear-weapon State party to the non-proliferation Treaty or any comparable internationally binding commitment not to acquire nuclear explosive devices, except in the case of an attack on the United States, its territories or armed forces or its allies by such a State allied to a nuclear-weapon State or associated with a nuclear-weapon State in carrying out or sustaining the attack". (CD/139)

Appendix III

Characteristics of Some Important Nuclear-Weapon Systems

Nation	Designator or name	First in service	Range km.	Number deployed	Payload; warhead, CEP, notes
Long-range strategic bombers					
USA	B-52 C/D/E/F	1956	18 500	83	27 tons; bombs
	B-52 G/H	1959	20 000	265	34 tons; bombs, Hound Dog, SRAM
USSR	Mya-4 BISON[a]	1955	10 000	59	9 tons; bombs, AS-4
	Tu-95 BEAR	1956	12 500	100	18 tons; bombs, AS-3, AS-6
Air-launched strategic weapons					
USA	Bombs			n.a.[b]	Mt range
	Hound Dog	1961	1 000	400	ALCM; 1 x kt range[c]
	SRAM	1972	150	1 020	ALBM; 1 x kt range
USSR	Bombs			n.a.[d]	Mt range
	AS-3 KANGAROO	1961	650	(800)	ALCM; 1 x Mt range
	AS-4 KITCHEN	1962	700		ALCM; 1 x kt range
	AS-6 KINGFISH	1977	250	n.a.	n.a.
ICBM (intercontinental ballistic missiles)					
USA	Titan II	1962	11 500	54	1 x 5-10 Mt; CEP 1 300 m
	Minuteman II	1966	13 000	450	1 x 1-2 Mt; CEP 400 m
	Minuteman III conv.	1970	13 000	550	3 x 170 kt MIRV; CEP 300 m
	Minuteman III impr.	1979	13 000		3 x 350 kt MIRV; CEP 300 m

Nation	Designator or name	First in service	Range km.	Number deployed	Payload; warhead, CEP, notes
USSR	SS-9 SCARP	1966	12 000	8	1 x 10-20 Mt; CEP 1 000-1 300 m
	SS-11 mod 1	1966	10 500		1 x 1 Mt;
	SS-11 mod 2 conv.	1973	n.a.	520	1 x 1 Mt; } CEP 1 000-1 800 m
	SS-11 mod 3 conv.	1973	n.a.		3 x 200 kt MRV;
	SS-13 SAVAGE	1969	8 000	60	1 x 1 Mt; CEP 1 300 m
	SS-17 conv.	1977	n.a.	150	4 x 500 kt MIRV; CEP 300-600 m
	SS-18 mod 1 and 3	1976	10 000	300	1 x 10-20 Mt; CEP 1 000-2 500 m
	S-18 mod 2 conv.	1977	n.a.		8 x 500 kt MIRV; CEP 300-600 m
	S-19 conv.	1976	9 000	300	6 x 500 kt MIRV; CEP 300-450 m
China	CSS-3	1976	7 000	2?	n.a.

SSBN (submarines, ballistic missile-equipped, nuclear-powered)

Nation	Designator or name	First in service	Range km.	Number deployed	Payload; warhead, CEP, notes
USA	With Polaris A-3	1964		5	16 x A-3
	With Poseidon C-3 conv.	1970		27	16 x C-3
	With Trident C-4 conv.	1979		4	16 x C-4
	With Trident C-4	1980?		1	24 x C-4
USSR	YANKEE I-class	1968		29	16 x SS-N-6
	HOTEL III-conv. class	1972		1	6 x SS-N-8
	DELTA I-class	1973		12	12 x SS-N-8
	YANKEE II-class	1974		1	16 x SS-NX-17
	DELTA II-class	1976		11	16 x SS-N-8
	DELTA III-class	1978		9	16 x SS-N-18
France	With MSBS M-20	1977		4	16 x MSBS M-20
Britain	With Polaris A-3	1967		4	16 x Polaris A-3

Nation	Designator or name	First in service	Range km.	Number deployed	Payload; warhead, CEP, notes
SLBM (Submarine-launched ballistic missiles)e					
USA	Polaris A-3	1964	4 600	80	3 x 200 kt MRV; CEP 900 m
	Poseidon C-3	1970	4 600	432	10 x 40 kt MIRV; CEP 500 m
	Trident C-4	1979	7 500	88	8 x 100 kt MIRV; CEP 500 m
USSR	SS-N-6 mod 1	1968	2 400	464	1 x 1 Mt;
	SS-N-6 mod 2 conv.	1973	2 900		1 x 1 Mt; } CEP 1 000–2 500 m
	SS-N-6 mod 3 conv.	1973	2 900		2 x 200 kt MRV;
	SS-N-8	1973	7 900	326	1 x 1 Mt; CEP 1 000–1 500 m
	SS-NX-17	n.a.	n.a.	16	1 x 1 Mt (MIRV-cap.); CEP n.a.
	SS-N-18	n.a.	7 500	144	3 x 200 kt MIRV; CEP 550–1 000 m
France	MSBS M-20	1977	4 800	64	1 x 1 Mt. CEP n.a.
Britain	Polaris A-3	1967	4 600	64	3 x 200 kt MRV; CEP n.a.
ABM (anti-ballistic missile system)					
USSR	ABM-1 GALOSH	1967	300	64	1 x kt range
LRCM (long-range cruise missiles)					
USSR	SS-N-3 SHADOCK	1962	700	100	1 x kt range; deployed on cruisers and submarines
Medium-range bombersf					
USA	FB-111	1970	6 000	65	17 tons; SRAM
USSR	Tu-16 BADGER	1955	7 500	613	9 tons; bombs
	Tu-22M BACKFIRE	1975	7 500	72	9 tons; bombs, AS-4, AS-6
Britain	Vulcan B2	1960	7 500	48	10 tons
China	Tu-16	n.a.	7 500	(<300)g	n.a.
	Tu-4	n.a.	7 500		n.a.

Nation	Designator or name	First in service	Range km.	Number deployed	Payload; warhead, CEP, notes
IRBM, MRBM (intermediate-/medium-/range ballistic missiles)					
USSR	SS-4 SANDAL	1959	1 900	500	1 x 1 Mt; obsolescent
	SS-5 SKEAN	1961	3 700	90	1 x 1 Mt; obsolescent
	SS-20	1977	4 000	120	3 x 150 kt MIRV; CEP 300 m
France	SSBS S-2	1971	3 000	18	1 x 150 kt
China	CSS-2	n.a.	2 600	50–70	n.a.
	CSS-1	n.a.	1 000	40–50	n.a.
SRBM (short-range ballistic missiles)					
USA	Lance	1972	110	36	1 x kt range; 54 further weapons are deployed by Belgium, Britain, the Federal Republic of Germany, Italy and the Netherlands
	Pershing	1962	700	108	1 x kt range; 72 further weapons are deployed by the Federal Republic of Germany
	Honest John	1953	40	0	1 x kt range; 91 weapons are deployed by the Federal Republic of Germany, Greece and Turkey

Nation	Designator or name	First in service	Range km.	Number deployed	Payload; warhead, CEP, notes
USSR	FROG-7	1965	70		1 x kt range; Also deployed by all Warsaw Pact nations
	SS-1b SCUD A	1957	80	1 300	1 x kt range; " " " "
	SS-1c SCUD B	1965	300		1 x kt range; " " " "
	SS-12 SCALEBOARD	1969	800		1 x Mt range; " " " "
France	Pluton	1974	120	32	1 x 15–25 kt
Artillery					
USA	M-110 203 mm how.	1962	15		1 x kt range; Deployed by most NATO nations
	M-109 155 mm how.	1964	15		1 x kt range;
USSR	M-55 203 mm gun–how.	1950s	30		Availability of nuclear shells not confirmed
Strike aircraft†					
USA	F-4 C/D/E	1962	2 200	390 in Europe	7 tons
	F-N1 A/E	1967	4 700		13 tons
	F-4 J/N	1962	2 200	100 in Europe	7 tons; Carrier-based
	A-6 E	1963	3 200		8 tons; Carrier-based
	A-7 E	1966	4 500		9 tons;

Nation	Designator or name	First in service	Range km.	Number deployed	Payload; warhead, CEP, notes
USSR	Il-28 BEAGLE	1950	2 200		2 tons
	Su-7 FITTER A	1959	1 450		2 tons; Also deployed by Czechoslovakia and Poland
	Tu-22 BLINDER	1962	2 200	3 500	5 tons
	MiG-21 FISHBED	1970	1 850		1 ton
	MiG-27 FLOGGER	1971	1 450		3 tons
	Su-20 FITTER C	1974	1 770		5 tons; Also deployed by Poland
	Su-19 FENCER	1974	1 450		4 tons
NATO	F-104	1958	2 400		4 tons; Most NATO nations
	F-4	1962	2 200		7 tons; Britain, the Federal Republic of Germany, Greece, Turkey
	Buccaneer	1962	3 700	50	5 tons; Britain
	Jaguar	1974	1 600		5 tons; Britain
France	Mirage IV A	1964	3 200	33	7 tons
	Jaguar	1974	1 600		5 tons

Sources: SIPRI Yearbook 1980, *Tactical Nuclear Weapons* (SIPRI 1978), *The Military Balance, 1979–1980* (IISS).

a. NATO code-names for Soviet weapons are given in capital letters.

b. Not available.

c. Number x yield.

d. Figure uncertain.

e. United States SLBMs considered inoperative due to current conversion to Trident not included.

f. Some of these aircraft may have a conventional rather than a nuclear role. In many cases it is also not clear which types of nuclear weapons they would carry. SIPRI classification of Mirage IV A is "strike aircraft".

g. About 90 Tu-16 in the strategic forces, according to Military Balance.

Notes

.

1 Subsequently referred to as the Group of Experts on a Comprehensive Study on Nuclear Weapons.

2 Originally published in 1968 (United Nations publication, Sales No. E.68.IX.1), this work was later reprinted in *Basic Problems of Disarmament* (United Nations publication, Sales No. 70.I.14).

3 *Nuclear Proliferation Factbook*, prepared by the Congressional Research Service, Library of Congress, United States Government Printing Office, 23 September 1977, p. 382.

4 Figures pertaining to numbers and characteristics of weapons quoted in this chapter are based on data given in *SIPRI Yearbook 1980* or *The Military Balance* (1979–1980), International Institute for Strategic Studies, London, unless otherwise stated.

5 As at 12 July 1980 this treaty had not been ratified.

6 Note that this chapter uses primarily the Western designators for both United States and Soviet missiles because they have long been familiar under those titles and because Soviet designators are generally not published. The correspondence between Soviet and NATO designators for Soviet missiles specified in the SALT II treaty is as follows: RS–16 = SS–77; RS–18 = SS–19; RS–20 = SS–18; RSM–50 = SS–N–18.

7 Whereas "battlefield" usually refers only to the zone of ground combat, "theatre" encompasses rear areas containing for instance air bases, reserve forces and supply depots. In some cases, a corresponding distinction is made between "tactical" and "theatre" weapons. This distinction is now upheld in this report.

8 Figures quoted from "Tactical Nuclear Weapons: European Perspectives", edited by SIPRI (London, Taylor and Francis, 1978).

9 Some other works in the abundant literature on issues related to nuclear

proliferation have also been used in preparing this section. Of particular importance is the report entitled "Nuclear Proliferation and Safeguards" by the Congress of the United States (Office of Technology Assessment, 1977).

10 Among the sources drawn upon in the preparation of this chapter, some of the most comprehensive and authoritative are the following:

(a) Hearings before a Subcommittee of the Committee on Appropriations, United States Senate, 96th Congress, First Session, Part Four, Department of Defense Appropriations for Fiscal Year 1980;

(b) Hearings before the Committee on Armed Services, United States Senate, 96th Congress, First Session, Part Six, Research and Development;

(c) Hearings on Military Posture, Department of Defense Authorization for Appropriations for Fiscal Year 1980 before the Committee on Armed Services, House of Representatives, 96th Congress, Part Three.

11 *Effects of a comprehensive test ban treaty on United States national security interests.* Hearings before the Panel on the Strategic Arms Limitation Talks and the Comprehensive Test Ban Treaty of the Intelligence and Military Application of Nuclear Energy Subcommittee of the Committee on Arms Services, House of Representatives, 95th Congress, Second Session, August 1978.

12 *Prospect for a comprehensive nuclear test ban treaty.* Hearings for the Subcommittee on Arms Control, International Law and Organization of the Committee on Foreign Relations, United States Senate, 92nd Congress, First Session on a comprehensive nuclear test ban treaty, July 1971.

13 Glasstone, S. and Dolan, P. J., *The Effects of Nuclear Weapons,* 3rd ed., 1977.

14 "The Effects of Nuclear War", Office of Technology Assessment of the Congress of the United States, Washington, D.C., 1979.

15 Glasstone and Dolan, *op. cit.*

16 Numerical estimates of casualties, etc., in this and the following section were made at the Swedish National Defense Research Institute.

17 This 3:1 relationship can be found in many military works published during the last 50 years. A recent reference is United States Army Field Manual FM 100-5: Operations.

18 With a given population density and average shielding factor, the number of casualties is almost directly proportional to the fission yield in surface bursts. For instance, with 100 persons/km^2 and an average shielding factor of 0.3, there would be about 70 early radiation deaths per kiloton fission yield exploded close to the ground.

19 C. F. von Weizsäcker (ed.), *Kriegsfolgen und Kriegsverhütung,* Munich, 1971.

20 R. Sullivan, *et al., Civil Defense Needs of High-Risk Areas of the United States,* System Planning Corporation, Arlington, Va., SP 409, 1979.

21 A. Katz, "Economic and Social Consequences of Nuclear Attacks on the United States", United States Senate, Committee on Banking, Housing and Urban Affairs, 96th Congress, First Session (March 1979).

22 The concept of "equivalent megatonnage" has been introduced to take account of the fact that the area covered by blast does not increase linearly with weapon yield. It is defined as the 2/3 power of the actual yield expressed in Mt. For instance, if the yield is 100 kt. = 0.1 Mt., then the equivalent megatonnage is $0.1^{2/3} = 0.22$. See also figure II in chap. II.

23 (a) "Data Base and Damage Criteria for Measurements of Arms Limitation Effects on War Supporting Industry", ACDA/WEC-242, 1974.

(b) Office of Technology Assessment, op. cit.

(c) G. Kemp, "Nuclear Force for Medium Powers, Part I. Targets and Weapon Systems, Part II and III. Strategic Requirements and Options"; Adelphi Papers 106 and 107, International Institute for Strategic Studies, London, 1974.

24 United States Senate, Committee on Banking, Housing and Urban Affairs, op. cit.

25 See, for instance, "Long Term Worldwide Effects of Multiple Nuclear-Weapons Detonations", National Academy of Sciences, Washington, D.C., 1975.

26 Krakatoa is a small volcanic island in the Sunda Straits which was almost completely blown to pieces by underwater explosions when the volcano erupted in August 1883. This is the largest recorded volcanic event.

27 The total production of grains in the world is equivalent to about 365 kg. per person and year while the minimum subsistence level is somewhere between 200 and 250 kg., unless complementary diet is available. However, the annual production per capita is very different in different regions, running from a high of more than 1,200 kg. in North America to a low of less than 150 kg. in Africa. The figures are for 1976 according to the FAO Production Yearbook, 1977.

28 Sources and Effects of Ionizing Radiation (United Nations publication, Sales No. E.77.IX.1).

29 For ^{14}C which has a very long half-life (5,730 years), only doses accumulated up to the year 2000 have been included. In total it would add a dose of 240 millirad delivered over some 10,000 years.

30 Gretchko, The Armed Forces of the Soviet State, p. 272.

31 R. Aron, "Initiations à la stratégie atomique", Le Monde, 14 November 1963, p. 3.

32 Department of State Bulletin, vol. 30, 25 January 1954, pp. 107–110.

33 This concept was used both by United States Secretary of Defense McNamara and by General Norsted within NATO.

34 Speech delivered at Ann Arbor, Michigan, on 16 June 1962.

35 Survival, vol. XVII, No. 1 (January-February 1975).

36 Statement of Secretary of Defense Harold Brown, on 25 January 1979, Survival, vol. XXI, No. 3 (May–June 1977).

37 Statement of Secretary Brown, "The New US Defense Program", *Survival*, vol. XIX, No. 3 (May—June 1977).

38 *Pravda*, 15 January 1960.

39 *Pravda*, 25 October 1961.

40 V. D. Sokolovsky, *Soviet Military Strategy*, English translation, MacDonald and Jane's, London, 1975, p. 195.

41 *Ibid.*, p. 208.

42 *Ibid.*, p. 288.

43 A. S. Zjoltov, *Militärische Theorie und Militärische Praxis*, Berlin, 1972.

44 Gretchko, *op. cit.*, pp. 348 and 349.

45 Baylis, Booth, Garnett and Williams, *Contemporary Strategy, Theories and Policies*, London, 1975, p. 260.

46 Mao Tsetung, "Imperialists and All Reactionaries Are Paper Tigers", *Current Background*, No. 534, 12 November 1958, p. 8.

47 Powell, "Maoist Military Doctrine", *Asian Survey*, April 1968.

48 *Livre blanc sur la défense nationale*, Tome I, 1972, p. 8.

49 The United States, the Soviet Union, the United Kingdom, France and China. India conducted a peaceful explosion in 1974 demonstrating a capability to construct nuclear weapons. The Government of India has repeatedly stated that India has no intention of constructing nuclear weapons. Israel and South Africa have denied unofficial reports that they have constructed nuclear weapons.

50 It has often been stated that the optimum number of weapons delivered against soft targets (civilian centres and industrial complexes) to provide a threat of assured destruction is around 400. The figure is a function of the mass destruction capability of the weapons and the limited number of large population centres and industrial complexes in the adversary State.

51 *SIPRI Yearbook, 1977*.

52 Table III, Final Report of Working Group Four—Reprocessing, Plutonium Handling and Recycle, International Nuclear Fuel Cycle Evaluation.

53 Some 60 States have so far signed safeguards agreements with IAEA.

54 Nuclear-weapon States parties to the Treaty are not required to place their nuclear facilities under safeguards. The United Kingdom and the United States have, however, voluntarily offered to accept safeguards on non-military facilities. A principal obligation under the terms of the Treaty for nuclear-weapon States is to reverse the nuclear arms race and negotiate disarmament measures. A number of States have refused to accede to the Treaty because the obligations to be assumed by nuclear and non-nuclear-weapons States are not equal.

55 Egypt, India, Israel, South Africa and Spain. Egypt, which has signed but not ratified the Treaty, operates a small research reactor provided under Soviet safeguards. Spain operates a power reactor jointly with France. There have been reports that Pakistan is constructing an unsafeguarded enrichment facility.

Pakistan has stated that its nuclear programme is peaceful.

56 The Nuclear Suppliers Group—Belgium, Canada, Czechoslovakia, France, Germany, Federal Republic of, the German Democratic Republic, Italy, Japan, the Netherlands, Poland, Sweden, Switzerland, the USSR, the United Kingdom and the United States—notified IAEA in 1978 of common guidelines to be applied in the export of nuclear material equipment or technology.

57 *SIPRI Yearbook, 1980.*

58 It is of interest to note here that subsurface bursts are more efficient than surface bursts in crater creating and underground damage. Hence earth-penetrating devices of very high precision can be quite damaging to fortified underground structures even with yields as "small" as of the order of a few kt.

59 Recommendations of the International Commission on Radiological Protection, ICRP Publication 26, 1977.

DATE DUE

DEMCO 38-296